MAY 0 8 2019

D1505668

FIDM Library
55 Stockton Street
San Francisco, CA 94108

PERFECT WEDDING • PERFECT STYLE

BIG DAY

Perfect Wedding • Perfect Style

First published and distributed by
viction:workshop ltd.

viction:ary™

viction workshop ltd.
Unit C, 7/F, Seabright Plaza, 9-23 Shell Street,
North Point, Hong Kong
Url: www.victionary.com   Email: we@victionary.com

 @victionworkshop
 @victionary_
 @victionworkshop

Edited and produced by viction:ary
Concepts & art direction by Victor Cheung
Book design by viction:workshop ltd.
Showcase text by Katee Hui

Cover image & facing page image courtesy of Maïlys
Fortune Photography & Gregory Batardon
Big Day title lettering by Sharon Tan

©2018 viction workshop ltd.
All rights reserved. No part of this publication may be
reproduced, stored in retrieval systems or transmitted in
any form or by any means, electronic, mechanical, pho-
tocopying, recording or any information storage, without
written permissions from respective copyright owner(s).

Copyright on text and design work is held by respective
designers and contributors. All artwork and textual information in this book are based on the materials offered
by designers whose work has been included. While every
effort has been made to ensure their accuracy, vic-
tion:workshop does not accept any responsibility, under
any circumstances, for any errors or omissions.

ISBN 978-988-77746-9-3
Printed and bound in China

Big Day

viction:ary

"No two weddings are ever the same, no two couples are. Then add to that, the fact that traditions vary from culture to culture, you have a job where no two days ever seem the same either."

—

Siobhan Craven-Robins

I was delighted to be asked to write the foreword for Victionary's first 'dabble' into the world of weddings! Whilst it may seem a somewhat saturated market, I would beg to differ. Weddings are, by their very nature, an inspirational, aspirational and visually stimulating event. Couples look for inspiration from many avenues: travel, dining out, décor, traditions, to name just some of them. I think that is why books such as this, that include a mix of helpful tips, advice and beautiful imagery can prove invaluable to many couples planning their weddings.

When I first started my wedding planning business is 1996, there were hardly any books that focussed on weddings. I can recall being so excited when Martha Stewart, Colin Cowie and Preston Bailey almost simultaneously released glossy hardbacks filled with creative imagery and advice in the late 90s. It was a window into the work of talented individuals and styles outside of the UK. Now, there are many such publications, and I think this is a good thing. Industry creatives such as florists and cake designers have started to release books on a regular basis, showcasing their work and techniques. This all helps to maintain a thriving industry and celebrates the talent within it.

Having worked in the wedding world for 21 years now, I have seen a cacophony of talent, incredible work and true artistry. I think that it can often go unrecognised in our industry, it's created for one day, then torn down and committed to memory only in the photos that are held by those involved. It seems an awful waste. I think our industry is one to celebrate and the talent should be recognised and credited. Books like this, do just that...

One of the things I love about being a part of this industry is the diversity, no two weddings are ever the same, no two couples are. Then add to that, the fact that traditions vary from culture to culture, you have a job where no two days ever seem the same either. There is much to explore and learn and I feel that I never stop learning. Couples' heritage and culture provide much of the inspiration for a wedding day, but in our cosmopolitan world, many times couples are not marrying in their home country, let alone their home town and so the wedding takes on an identity all of its own that blends the many influences. I think that this is what makes them even more of a celebration, they act as a marker in an ever-changing world and represent the right now.

My advice to couples as they start planning their wedding is to keep it authentic, design something that celebrates who you are together, and apart, and where you've come from – you are a unique coupling and your day will reflect this. Keeping it authentic also eliminates it becoming contrived or quickly dated, it is a representation of you, your heritage, and the celebration you want to have to mark this important stage in your lives.

I am sure you will find much inspiration and advice in the following pages; don't be afraid to adapt ideas that grab you to make them your own. Couples can often fear being limited by their budget. Whilst a big budget can accommodate more guests, finer wines and a more elaborate setting, it does not naturally create a sincere and joyous occasion — this is down to you, your friends and family, and your vision for your celebration. Note anything you like and then talk to the relevant supplier on how this can be adapted for your wedding. You are hiring the most creatives you will probably ever hire for one event in your life — use them, challenge them and be open to their ideas — it will make for a most enjoyable planning process for all of you and create a most wonderful celebration for you and your special guests.

Good luck and ENJOY!

Starting her business in 1996, Siobhan Craven-Robins is one of the original wedding planners in the UK. She has been frequently invited to comment and offer tips on planning the perfect wedding on national radio and television, and lend her expertise to various bridal publications.

All you need is love, love is all you need.

Alison & Bryan | Wedding planners

Alison Laesser-Keck and Bryan Keck are destination wedding and event planners based in Santa Barbara, California. For over a decade, the husband-and-wife team has woven over 200 narratives of people and love, at familiar and out-of-ordinary locations for those who wish to share their joy as they journey toward becoming man and wife. From the United States to Europe, forest to ballroom, they take pride in turning dreams into reality, grabbing the interest of *Vogue*, *Harper's Bazaar*, and *Elle Italia*. Vivid travellers themselves, with a solid background in hospitality, the couple keeps their hands busy running the full spectrum from concept to completion with a creative spirit. *Portrait by Trevor Pikhart*.

HAPPY
PLANNING!

WHAT IT TAKES TO CREATE A PERFECT WEDDING

in style?

by

— Alison & Bryan —

Photographed by Chasewild

Start with a Plan

Most couples getting married today are looking for a much more personal and custom experience than what their parents had for their weddings. Consumers have so many options in general these days, and their wedding is no exception. There are so many different types of weddings one can have based on location, aesthetic, and the type of guest experience they're aspiring to have. Couples today are able to match their preferences and personalities with the hotel, restaurant, and travel destination that is right for them. So when it comes to one of the biggest and most emotional purchases of their life, they want that same bespoke experience and personal approach for their wedding.

Planning a wedding can be really intense and overwhelming at times for those who are engaged. It can be enough to worry about with the basics of finding a venue and the right vendors to work with, that most can't even begin to think about the aesthetics without getting stressed out. Combine that with the fact that costs can be exorbitant and everything adds up, there's so much to navigate and people can quickly feel overwhelmed.

With there being so many options for those getting married, the most important thing is to really think about who you are and what you want as a couple, and then create a budget and roadmap around those wishes and stick to it. If you do too much in the beginning without thinking things through, it can really limit you and force you into decisions you might not necessarily want to make for the rest of the planning process. Don't get us wrong, there's nothing wrong with wanting to splurge on an amazing photographer or venue right off the bat if it's something that is really important to you, but it's critical to look at the big picture and ask yourself how it will fit in with the rest of the moving parts. You can have the best photographer or florist in the world, but if you didn't leave enough in your budget for lighting those installations and centrepieces, all of those gorgeous flowers will disappear when the sun goes down. Booking a venue without really knowing what the pros and cons can really pigeonhole you (and cost you). It's all about balance, and creating a proper plan before you make any decisions is key.

We like to think of planning a wedding as similar to building a house from scratch. You take your plot of land, fully assess the budget (a realistic budget that is based on your needs and goals), create some plans, and start building. You wouldn't start picking paint colours before you have flooring. You also wouldn't pick out the style of your bathtub before you do a build out to attend to the overall functionality of the space.

"The details are not the details; they are the design."

Approach As Designers

We are very similar to most of our clients in that we share a love for travel, adventure, and the details in design. A favourite quote of ours is a well-known one from Charles Eames that says, "The details are not the details; they are the design." A great wedding has the same attention to detail as a great hotel. From the font of the hotel signage to the products in the rooms, the lighting and textures of fabrics in the common areas, and even the styling of uniforms for staff should be cohesive and speak to who the guest is and what the overall experience you're creating is.

You can get a quick idea of where you want to go aesthetically by being honest with yourself about where you love to travel, what they like about your favourite places to stay, or even the kind of restaurant experiences you love. What is it about those brands that draw you in? Are you drawn to the simple elegance of places like Italy, where the style can feel relaxed and understated, yet still polished and sophisticated? Or do you feel more comfortable in the exquisite surroundings of a magical city like Paris, with its Rococo and Art Nouveau styling that are more opulent? There's a reason people connect to these things emotionally, and if you can understand that, it can really help give you some insight into what direction you should take in designing your event.

Things that inspire us when we design an event are actually not other weddings, but design and overall cultural experiences in general. What happens when you travel to Italy? Food is big. Flowers appear to be growing on homes in unique ways. There is a connection from the interior to the exterior of a space. Everything is simple, approachable, and charming. Limoncello is served in cute little glasses following a meal. It is much more than a digestif; it is a tradition. These types of things that places like Italy are known for serve a greater purpose than people realise. It becomes a refuge. There is a reason why people holiday there. It is consistent. It is comfortable. It feels like a home.

We believe a good event capitalises on that kind of experience. What your guests wear, how they travel from space to space, what they eat, what they drink, the presentation of it all — we can go on forever, but when you pay attention to those details, it has an affect on overall mood and guest comfortability and enjoyment. Ambience, cohesiveness and consistency takes what's expected to be a typical cookie-cutter experience, to an experience that is completely once in a lifetime. The attention to detail then becomes something incredibly special and groundbreaking. We've seen our clients and their guests get brought to tears off ambience alone.

Designed by Kelly Verstraeten

STATIONERY DESIGN

One of the most important and easily overlooked area of events is graphic design. It's easy to find an invitation suite that's "pretty", and is competent when it comes to giving your guests the info they need while also being aesthetically pleasing as a standalone invite. It's also very effective to print up nice escort cards in a beautiful font for guest seating. Does it get your guests excited though? Does it build suspense about this experience they are going to be taken through with you? That invitation a guest receives sets the tone and tints the view of how your guests will approach and experience your event. Having a graphic designer create a custom pattern for your invitations, and then weaving it into the backdrops, napkins, lighting projections, or custom linens, is a way to provide strong attention to detail and make your guests feel like they have been transported to a different world, wherever your event happens to take place. One of our favourite ways to communicate with guests is through custom illustration. Instead of listing a cocktail and its ingredients in a bar menu, why not have an artist paint

a cute little watercolor versions of each drink. The guests have already been reading invitations and welcome booklets and programs, let's show them what you're offering and get them excited to explore and enjoy themselves.

Another great way to surprise your guests and set that tone is to use unique materials and printing methods for your invitations and day of material. Using leather, metal, wood, plants, really anything that better communicates the feel of your event cohesively, is a way to give guests the information they need while keeping them excited. In the past, we've hand-lettered the husks of ears of corn for seating at a farm venue, and brought in seaglass with calligraphed escort cards on the shore of Lake Michigan. As long as it matches the aesthetics and energy of the venue and the couple, and it works logistically, those times when you need to communicate with your guests are great opportunities to think outside of the box and elevate the guest experience.

"Let's show them what you're offering and get them excited to explore and enjoy themselves."

"It's just so paramount to share these stories, because without them your guests will miss out on so much of the personality of yours."

IDENTITY & BRANDING

We've talked about the different layers of design we use to pull guests into an event. Just as important as the story itself though, is the context of that story for your guests. Things like the emotional or historical significance of a venue, or maybe the date or time of year chosen for the event can really add colour to that story. We've had clients who have chosen a church that their parents, grandparents, and great-grandparents have all gotten married in. Or maybe a bride and groom are choosing a family estate where so many generations of family grew up in and created special memories. We had also once created a long pathway to a ceremony where we invited guests to "walk the story". On the side of the pathway were stories and photos displayed chronologically of small and large moments from the beginning of their relationship leading up to their wedding day. At the end of the walk was the ceremony space, marking the end of one chapter (dating) and the beginning of another (marriage).

It's just so paramount to share these stories, because without them your guests will miss out on so much of the personality of yours. All of these pieces are important on their own, and when combined they allow guests to become connected to the story in ways they otherwise wouldn't be able to. It's a way of communicating your identity as a couple in the most authentic and honest possible manner. From there, it's that much more special and personal.

Photographed by Pippa Mackenzie, courtesy of Siobhan Craven-Robins

FLORAL ARRANGEMENT

When most couples begin to think about what they want their wedding to look like, nine out of ten times their thoughts will start with flowers. With good reason, as the delicate texture, washes of colour and soft fragrance can immediately invoke feelings of sentimentality and romanticism in most any guest. Flowers can be very fickle though, and with that delicate nature comes the necessity for gentle care. Extreme heat, direct sun or sitting too long of a time without water can wreak havoc on your investment, so it's important to hire an experienced floral designer who has an understanding of the climate and infrastructure of your venue's surroundings. So how do we incorporate flowers into an event that goes beyond the basic idea of lovely floral arrangements on tables during dinner? One of our favourite ways to add to the narrative is through 'curated floral installations'. Whether it be a long organic floral piece that is suspended over a head table or a floral wall backdrop for an amazing jazz band, these larger statement pieces can connect with those smaller floral arrangements and make things feel a bit more experiential. Many times cocktails, dinner, and then dancing are all happening in different spaces. So instead of putting all of your floral budget into table arrangements for two hours of attention during the meal, consider spreading out that budget to smaller table top arrangements and the cool floral backdrop for your cocktail bar to connect things better aesthetically and let that energy flow through the night. Having floral pieces of varying scales also helps break up the monotony of duplicate arrangements that, while beautiful, can kind of desensitise your guests and blend together, diminishing the impact that they could have brought to the venue.

LIGHTING

Most clients don't think about lighting being so crucial to an event, but bang for your buck, there's no better way to transform a space and enhance the ambience of a party. One of the most important advantages of great lighting is the ability to highlight special moments and distract the eye. Most couples will mention how much they dislike the carpet or curtains in a room when they first tour a space, but once we turn the venue's lighting off and pinspot the important areas like floral and tabletops, you and your guests' eyes will be drawn to the table and that awful carpet disappears in the shadows. Projection is also becoming an important area of social events in the industry today. Taking a custom floral pattern and projecting it on the walls of a ballroom, or the ceiling of a loft, can create visual interest and really capture your guests' attention and bring in that wow factor.

Photographed by Raquel Benito Photography

TABLESCAPES

Tabletop design is another important aspect of a wedding, not just aesthetically but functionally as well. Sitting down and having a meal at a table with seven other people you may have never met before can be awkward. And having centrepieces or other decoration that gets in your way of talking or saying "cheers!" can really separate guests during dinner. Family style dinners are really popular for weddings today, and all of those platters and serving bowls, no matter how beautifully curated they are, can take up a lot of room for your guests. Are your tables large and spacious enough for a family style meal to be comfortably enjoyed? Think about those small round tables you walk past at Parisian cafés where people are enjoying a nice espresso or croissant. They're absolutely adorable, but horribly small if you're having a proper lunch. For most, it doesn't matter, it's charming and well, you're in Paris! But when you have 200 guests, not everyone is charmed by being crowded with everyone at their table. So, make it not only beautiful, but comfortable and enjoyable for every guest to mingle or simply eat.

FOOD & BEVERAGE

What you serve in this environment that you've created, especially the way you present it, is another crucial part in keeping guests engaged. Playful food and drink pairings that bring in local culture and make a connection to the community or regional traditions make for a fantastic option. What can you give your guests there that they can't have anywhere else? If I'm getting married in Indonesia, I want the indigenous produce and fruits that you can't find in Santa Barbara, recipes that locals have been cooking for hundreds of years to be featured and shine through in the meal. Maybe there's an incredible locally-brewed rice wine that you could create cocktails with and make the drinks unique. And you don't need to have a sit-down, plated dinner. Interactive food stations like oyster bars in Maine, or maybe an open grill with a chef serving elote while in Mexico, can keep guests engaged and create a different energy to connect cocktail hour and dancing. Not only will it be unique and fun, but potentially also be more affordable in the end. It's not necessarily about feeding your guests the fanciest meal, because everyone can have the perfect filet and expensive wine. Guests have seen that a hundred times and I'm sure they will see it many more, but they might only have one chance to go to your destination. So push that caterer and planner and make it count!

Photographed by Chasewild

Photographed by Raquel Benito Photography

CONNECTING PARTS

Once you have all of the pieces of an event put into place, the last thing you need to do is to connect everything so that you can accomplish the things you want to happen in a timely manner, while making it feel as honest and spontaneous as possible. Any experienced planner will have a timeline that is insanely detailed and airtight, but if they do their job well, the event will feel as effortless and natural to every guest there.

Once you get guests emotionally involved in an event, you want to do everything you can to keep them in that world, sharing it with their friends and family. The flowers, lighting, food and music can be perfect, but if there's a lag in timing or guests become conscious of "the event", you can really lose that energy that takes a wedding to the next level.

What we see for the future

We really see weddings continuing down the road of quality over quantity. Couples are choosing smaller guest counts with just close family and friends, and choosing more intimate and unique environments for their venues. With fewer guests attending and needing to travel, it also makes a destination wedding more of an option for people. You can have your wedding in one of your hometown venues that you've been to a hundred weddings at before, or you can treat yourselves and your guests to an amazing experience in Europe or South America that is something new and different which they'll be so excited to share with you. We're definitely seeing grooms taking more care and interest into their events, especially with destination weddings. A ballroom filled with flowers doesn't get most guys excited, but the

opportunity to take your family and friends to Lake Como for an amazing adventure to celebrate... I'm in! And that adventurousness is really becoming more apparent with brides too, specifically with fashion. Multiple dress and outfit changes throughout the day are pretty common now. This really allows a girl to take a chance and maybe wear something a little more fashion forward and a little less functional for the ceremony. You can always change into that cute little dress to relax and dance later in the evening, so why not go for it? I think we're seeing a lot of the tradition and rigidity in the past with weddings being either passed over, or changed and tweaked to fit a couple. Do what you love! In the end, that is all that matters.

ographed by Raquel Benito Photography

Photographed by Luke Liable Photography

THE MOMENTS

Warehouse Union
CHASEWILD PHOTOGRAPHY

Romance in Venice
MAÏLYS FORTUNE PHOTOGRAPHY & GREGORY BATARDON

Kyoto Love in Blossom
MARTIN AESTHETICS LIMITED

In Wilderness & The Vow
LUKE LIABLE PHOTOGRAPHY

Love in the Woods
CHEESINESS PHOTO

Downtown Love
CHASEWILD PHOTOGRAPHY

Bodasound
RAQUEL BENITO PHOTOGRAPHY

A Unicorn Walks Into a Hackney Pub
LOVE & ADVENTURES

Bohemian Rhapsody
CHEESINESS PHOTO

Scandinavian Love Affair
ERIN WHEAT CO.

Magical Cheshire Bash
THE CRAWLEYS

European Beach Wedding Flair
VITALY AGEEV PHOTOGRAPHY

Warehouse Union

CHASEWILD PHOTOGRAPHY

Given free rein to capture the candid, cheery moments of Laura and James' wedding bash, Chasewild went specifically after the small gestures of love. From their family home to the ceremony and lunch reception at an antique warehouse, the styling was aesthetically simple, providing a perfect backdrop and down-home casual charm that worked effortlessly right. Mutual trust brought about a special connection between pictures and people, achieving the vision the couple had for their wedding day.

Planning: Amanda Norwood | Venue: The Vitrine | Bride's dress: Rue de Seine | Bride's shoes: Carlson | Groom's suit: Crane Brothers | Make-up: Laura Williamson | Hair: Olette | Engagement ring: Gems in Remuera | Wedding bands: Zoe and Morgan | Flora: Leaf and Honey | Catering: Monday's Wholefoods | Cake: The Caker | Lounge furniture: Two Foxes Styling | Bar: The Boutique Bar

"We want things to be real, honest and authentic. We want our couples to feel as comfortable as possible so they can simply be themselves."

Romance In Venice

MAÏLYS FORTUNE PHOTOGRAPHY & GREGORY BATARDON

At the top destination for proposals, weddings and romantic getaways, Maïlys Fortune wanted to create a unique and aspirational look. Part photojournalism and part fine art, each photo is crafted around a scene; not too busy in the background so the couples and details of their big day remain the focus. A soft, dreamy look with consistent colours was the treatment for this staged shoot, revealing the romantic aura and ambience that Venice has on offer.

Event design: Ema Giangreco | Venue: Residence Palazzo Odoni | Bride's dress: Watters, Riki Dalal | Groom's vest: Poil de Chameau | Bracelet: L'Atelier de Sylvie | Flora: Fioreria San Rocco Eventi | Models: Flora Marchon, Jorge M. Oliveira

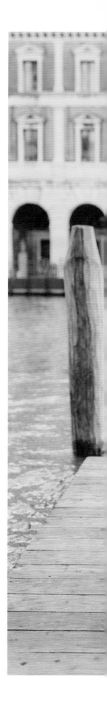

"It's mainly a question of light and choice of background. Our goal is to make them feel, live their day again through our pictures."

Kyoto Love in Blossom

MARTIN AESTHETICS LIMITED

—

A natural and urban environment set the scene for Nicole and Raymond's engagement photo shoot in Kyoto, with intermittent sunshine framing the day's shoot for the photographer. The philosophy that undermined the staging of the photos was that photography is a reflection of the heart. Gaining a deep understanding of the stories, the photographer wedded the brief to the couples' experiences and values that reflected the different faces and angles of love.

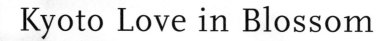

Makeup: Clarie Ho

"I will get to know them, suggest styles, try different light source, do something creative, and capture the most genuine expression of their love."

In Wilderness & The Vow

LUKE LIABLE PHOTOGRAPHY

Canadian photographer Luke Liable aims to create a lasting legacy in the photos he takes. By putting couples and their personalities as the main focus, he captures their stories and moments from the tiniest of interactions to big emotional displays. The balance between great lighting and location heed the best results and with Nolan and Davita's wedding on Vancouver Island, the scenic and wild environment provided the perfect stage.

Event Planner: Persimmon Tree Events | Bride's dress: Anna Campbell Bridal | Flora: Lisa Samphire |
Catering: Wits End Catering | DJ: djspeedyshoes.com

"For me, it's all about the clients and their story. If the photos represent the couple as who they are and what their love looks like then I have done my job."

BY SIOBHAN CRAVEN-ROBINS

Ways to set a realistic budget

Your perfect day will not necessarily be dictated by your spending parameters. However, as you start planning your wedding, you may discover expenses that you had not considered, such as special bridal underwear, wedding insurance (always advisable), or a catering service levy. It would be wise to pencil all possible expenses and costs from the outset. Make a spreadsheet of everything you want, all the wedding items you need, their estimated costs, and under each item, add in the extras. Go through this list to see what can be easily overlooked when first drafting your budget!

VENUE

SERVICE CHARGE — Usually levied if the venue is also providing the catering and isn't just a dry hire. Otherwise, you may want to tip some of your vendors.

SETUP & BREAKDOWN — If you are opting for a marquee, check if the venue charges hire on the days this will be set up and taken down.

DELIVERY & COLLECTION — If you hire furniture, lighting, or props, etc. for your wedding.

PHOTOGRAPHY & FILMING

PACKAGE ITEMS — Check if it includes all you want. For example, an album or as many copies of the DVD as you require.

TIME ALLOCATION — Most packages start at eight hours, which usually kick off from the point when the bride is getting ready, not when the ceremony begins.

OUTMESS COST – Don't forget all your suppliers and photographers need feeding and watering.

CAKE & CATERING

VAT. — Menu tasting charge, wine tasting charge. Some caterers may offer a free tasting for the two of you, but charge for any extra people.

CAKE — You will usually need a cake stand and knife. Check if this is something you have to hire or is provided by the venue.

CORKAGE — If you want to supply your own alcohol.

ATTIRE

BRIDE — Consider the extras such as bridal underwear, hair and makeup (including the trial), and possibly a flat pair of shoes for dancing!

FLOWERS

———

TRANSPORTATION & CLEARING — It's not just the bouquets, buttonholes and décor. There will usually be a charge for transport and for clearing.

GROOM — Often, during his speech, the groom will present bouquets to the mothers. If you wish to do this, ensure you order them with your florist and add them to your budget.

CEREMONY

———

CHOIR — There is usually a fee to the choir if you wish to film your religious ceremony. Some religious properties and/or officiants operate on a donation basis.

STATIONERY

———

POSTAGE — Ensure you include postage for your invitations and Save the Dates in your budget.

ORDER OF SERVICE — Programmes can be shared between people, so you don't need one for everyone.

PLACE CARDS — Double menus as place cards with the guest names printed or written on each one.

CALLIGRAPHY — If you want the names handwritten on place cards or menus, ensure you include calligraphy in the budget. Similarly, if you plan to have the invitation envelopes handwritten too.

TRANSPORT

———

SHUTTLE SERVICE — If your ceremony and reception venues are in two locations, you may want to consider supplying transport for your guests, particularly if parking is limited at either of them. You can choose one meeting point for the initial pick up and the end of evening drop off. Or, to keep costs down, guests can rely on taxis to get to the ceremony and home at the end of the night, but you provide transport between the two locations.

ENTERTAINMENT

———

SET TIMES — Prices quoted are usually for three hours (with breaks). Ensure that is enough to cover however long you want them to play or perform for.

LIGHTING — Not all bands come with lights, in which case you will need to hire additional lighting.

WEDDING FAVOURS

———

GIFTS — It is customary to give your wedding party gifts for playing a part in supporting you on your special day. Ensure you add these to the budget.

On top of everything else...

Your guest list is instrumental in working out an accurate budget. It is essential that you make this list first as you cannot accurately work out costs without knowing how many people you are catering for.

Be realistic from the outset: if you will be travelling on major roads to get to your ceremony location, a horse and carriage is not your ideal mode of transport! Similarly, if you are set on an outdoor wedding ceremony, choose a reliable month for fine weather but ALWAYS have a wet weather contingency plan.

In Wilderness & The Vow

CHEESINESS PHOTO

Choosing a densely forested part of Sequoia National Park as the location for the photo shoot, photographer Victor de la Cueva agreed with his client to have a campground vibe with a rustic feel. Despite heavy rain interrupting the shoot, the beauty of the natural setting and the couples' ability to relax in the woods created an atmospheric collection of photographs. Staged coloured smoke also contributed to the ambience and intrigue of the pictures.

Flora: Floweriize / Jimena Garduño

"Victor would always talk to the
couple before taking photos of them. He would also
asked them to play music they liked, bring their dogs
along, and just be playful and have fun."

Downtown Love

CHASEWILD PHOTOGRAPHY

—

Location is paramount to Chasewild and all wedding shoots they take on so that couples feel comfortable and be themselves. Using the streets of downtown Auckland as a backdrop for Joseph and Debbie's wedding, they roamed the streets with a fun and relaxed shoot with the bride sporting her traditional dress. As the day progressed the guests arrived at a stylish reception with touches of flora featuring throughout.

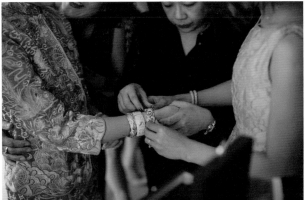

Venue: Everybody's Auckland

"We make sure the day is well planned, keep things light hearted and fun while allowing the couple the space to enjoy some intimate time on their wedding day."

Bodasound

RAQUEL BENITO PHOTOGRAPHY

Set in an underground factory with an alternative vibe, the photography for this DJ couple needed to reflect their shared passion for music and design to respect their personalities and spirit. The different factory elements combined with the illuminated space lit up with strings of lights gave an industrial feel and alternative edge, matching the photographs to the overall wedding theme to aptly capture Jessana and Ivan's day.

Planning: Bodas de Cuento | Illustration: Miaw | Catering:
Moncho's Catering

"Each couple has a defined personality, it's very important to respect it and create an atmosphere and style where they can recognise themselves when they receive the photos."

A Unicorn Walks Into
A Hackney Pub

LOVE & ADVENTURES

For Love & Adventures, the best weddings are those that discard tradition and embrace a joyful
creative expression of who the newlyweds are and the community they live in. This styled shoot in Hackney was
initiated to show the range of rich creative diversity in London's East End. The anarchic spirit and playfulness
shine through the photos through the narrative of rambunctious, neon rainbow stereotype-smashing party.

Art Direction & Styling: Cherelle Joseph (Perfectly Planned 4 You) | Venue: The Star By Hackney Downs | Bride's dress: Heart A Flutter | Groom's suit: Keye London | Millinery: Jodi McFayden | Make-up: Hackney Brides | Hair: Love Hair By Lou | Jewellery: Me & Zena | Flora: Shilpa Reddy | Stationery: Izzy | Biscuits: Emily Garland of Maid of Gingerbread | Models: Oma Benjamin, Ed Dyer

"[Good] pictures are more a narrative of a lovely moment, allowing the laughter and connection to emerge from between the couple."

Bohemian Rhapsody

CHEESINESS PHOTO

A beautiful couple is just one of the requirements needed for a memorable photo collection. For Cheesiness Photo, it's the combination of shooting in a breathtaking area of nature with accessories meaningful to the couple and complimentary added props like striking floral arrangements. The bride and groom were instructed to act normal around each other and be completely comfortable so that the emotions captured are real, not staged.

Flora: Floweriize / Jimena Garduño

"We would always encourage the couple
to be dressed up in their favourite clothes,
bring along accessories that they like and
represent their style."

TOP TIPS
for
A PERFECT WEDDING

BY SIOBHAN CRAVEN-ROBINS

Give yourself enough time

A wedding takes time to organise. A dress can take up to nine months to be made, popular venues often must be booked a good year in advance and invitations should ideally go out 6-8 weeks prior to the big day. Ensure that you have a realistic time period to plan your wedding and then you can enjoy all the preparation at a steady pace instead of in one mad rush!

As a general rule of thumb, there is an order in which to book your wedding suppliers.

Based on 12 months of planning:

9-10
- **Book a caterer** — if it's not in-house catering at your reception venue
- **Shop for a bridal gown**

8
- **Hire a florist**
- **Start planning the decor and look for party rentals** — such as props, furniture & lighting
- **Build your production team**
- **Make transportation arrangements**

6
- **Pick the groom, bridesmaids & ushers' attire**
- **Order your cake**
- **Choose your stationery**
- **Book a calligrapher (if needed)**

4
- **Order the wedding rings**

3
- **Extras —** Such as gifts for wedding party and favours

Wedding planner — Book one if you are hiring one!

Venue & ceremony venue — Do not confirm until you have contacted and confirmed whoever will officiate your ceremony. This particularly applies to venues where they use a registrar or officiant from an official body to conduct the ceremony.

Photographer, videographer, hair & makeup artists & entertainment — These suppliers can only take one wedding per date and if you have your heart set on someone, then book them early!

The sooner you book everything, the better. There is no definitive time plan, as it all depends on suppliers' availability and how long you have to plan your wedding. This is a practical order to book them in.

Scandinavian Love Affair

ERIN WHEAT CO.

A forestry fairy tale was the theme of this wedding, uniting the family background in Scandinavian culture in a serene woodland. Whilst the couple were getting ready, simple settings with as much negative space as possible were selected to remove all distractions from the photos. During the day, photographer Erin Wheat took the couple away from the festivities so they have time to settle in and connect with each other.

Venue: Foxfire Mountain House, Catskill Mountains, New York. | Bride's dress: Elizabeth Dye | Flora: Hops Petunia Floral | Design: Bride & Erin Wheat Co.

"Allowing clients a few moments to reconnect and settle can really make a world of difference in the images and the connection between the individuals."

Magical Cheshire Bash

THE CRAWLEYS

British photography team Bee and Liam have travelled the world, attending weddings to distill memories for people through photography. Liam's 'up close' documentary style of shooting is complimented by quirky portraits and shots at interesting angles of the couples, their guests and the surroundings. For Katy and Chris' funfair themed wedding, the Crawley's set out to produce something unique and full of personality.

Transport: Love Bus Wedding Company | Catering: Thyme Out, Smohk and Mischief | Tent: Papakata

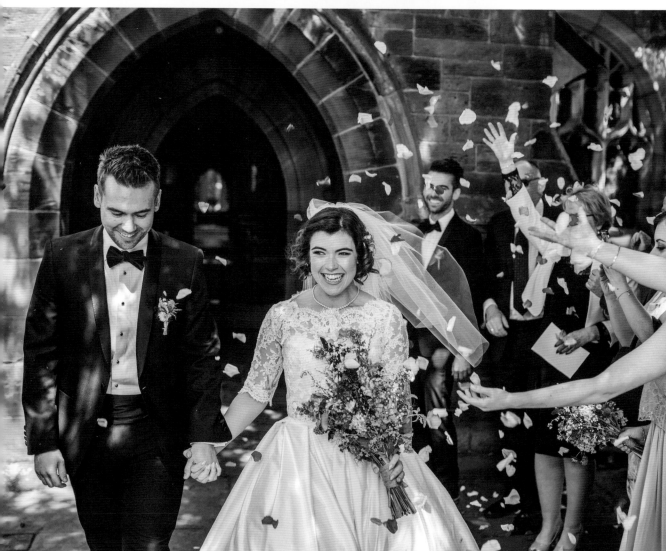

European Beach Wedding Flair

VITALY AGEEV PHOTOGRAPHY

A simple, paired back wedding with little decoration was key to creating an atmospheric and mellow collection of photographs for this collaborative project. Vitaly Ageev wanted to create the wedding of his dreams to showcase his work. Using warm light and maintaining a classical style for the shoot, including mandatory portraits informed his approach. The minimalistic design of the wedding, including the small guest list can be seen across the images conveying a relaxed and intimate sentiment in an idyllic location.

Planning & styling: Nostra Storia | Decor, floras & stationery: Renne Decor Studio | Bride's gown: Cathy Telle | Catering: Feola's Kitchen, Victoria Hairulina, Kate Miromova | Video: Big big day | Models: Success Russia

"I normally keep to the classical
style and focus on the couple's emotions and
relationships while trying to add something that
no one has ever done before. I like it when the
pictures have warm light and details that aren't
visible at first glance."

Suite Paperie
Kate & Tug's Miami Engagement Party

Coral Pheasant Stationery
Tropical Destination Wedding Invitation,
Modern Black & White

Kelly Verstraeten
Kelly & Stefan's Wedding Story

Gabriel Figueiredo & Gabriela Silva
Leca & Juliano,
Renê & Alex

Jacques & Lise
Tom & Karlien's Wedding Invitation

Julien Pradier
Capucine & Jerôme's wedding

Luminous Design Group
281214

Marie Pierer
Gemeinsam

Melissa Deckert
Danielle + Deane Save The Date

OlssønBarbieri
Karin+Sondre

ORIGIN.DESIGN studio
The Year in Love & Thanks

Pratic Design
Venetian Mystique

sincerely,
Olive Tree Wedding Card

X Spots The Mark
Off We Go

Emma Jo Stationery
Pencil Us In!
Harlow

Dream Giant Creative
Headstart for Happiness

El Calotipo

Juan & Laura

Ryan DePaola

DePaola Wedding Suite

Shipwright & Co.

Ashley & Mike,
Caitlin & Colin

A Fine Press

Copper Wedding Invitations,
Banyan Tree Invitation

Ho Ting-An

MOOC & CHIOU

Rachel Marvin Creative

Brenna Wedding Correspondence Set,
Southern Peach Wedding Correspondence Set,
Mae Wedding Correspondence Set,
Aurora Wedding Correspondence Set

Marta Sliwowska

M&K Wedding Invitation,
M&J Wedding invitation

studio of Christine Wisnieski

Wedding in Savannah,
Getting Hitched at a Football Stadium

Mondo Mombo

Meta & Albert

Shindig Bespoke

Jackie & Harry's,
Stephanie & Zack's Autumn Wedding,
Melissa & Greg's Vintage-inspired Wedding,
Daryl & Amir's New York Wedding,
Rebecca & Steve's Autumn Wedding
Chrissy & Tom's Boho Wedding

Abingo Wang

Wang & Cheng's Wedding Invitation

Idyll Paper

Champs De Fleurs,
Douceur

Atheneum Creative

Annabel & Jono

Studio Pros

Wedding Pass Set

Li Dyin

C&H Pop-Up Wedding Invitation

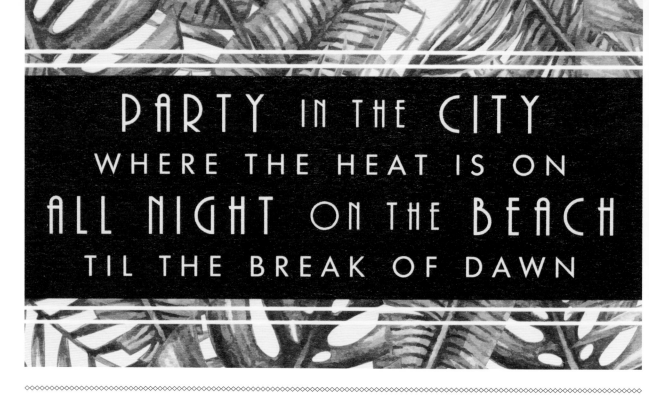

KATE & TUG'S MIAMI ENGAGEMENT PARTY

BY SUITE PAPERIE

The stylish invitation for Kate and Tug is explosively fun and screams "party" all the way. Growing up with 90s pop culture, the couple was inspired by Will Smith's "Miami". Each invite thus displays the stand-out lyric in Art Deco fonts, echoing the imagery of a wild summer party in tropical Florida. Saturated with tropical flora and an abundance of pink flamingos, the cards are completed with a rich colour palette of coral, teal, green, and black.

WE'RE ENGAGED!

COME PARTY WITH US

LOVE, KATE & TUG

THE RALEIGH HOTEL·MIAMI BEACH, FLORIDA

AUGUST 20TH · 7 O'CLOCK IN THE EVENING

PARTY IN THE CITY

WHERE THE HEAT IS ON

ALL NIGHT ON THE BEACH

TIL THE BREAK OF DAWN

WE'RE ENGAGED!

COME PARTY WITH US

LOVE, KATE & TUG

THE RALEIGH HOTEL·MIAMI BEACH, FLORIDA

AUGUST 20TH · 7 O'CLOCK IN THE EVENING

PARTY IN THE CITY

WHERE THE HEAT IS ON

ALL NIGHT ON THE BEACH

TIL THE BREAK OF DAWN

Photo: Lindsay Nathanson

TROPICAL DESTINATION WEDDING INVITATION

BY CORAL PHEASANT STATIONERY

A tribute to the bright and vibrantly coloured Barbados, these invitations feature watercolour leaves, illustrations and a gorgeous calligraphy juxtaposed with modern fonts and a fun language to top off its tropical vibes. Letterpress printed on double thick eggshell stock for the main invitation, it comes with a lattice-like design on the envelope liner and captures the essence of romance.

WELCOME DRINKS

REHEARSAL DINNER

WEDDING CEREMONY

WEDDING RECEPTION

FAREWELL BRUNCH

ALL THE DETAILS

MR. AND MRS. GARETH JOSEPH GREEN
REQUEST THE HONOR OF YOUR PRESENCE AT THE
MARRIAGE OF THEIR DAUGHTER

Jessica Mary Green
to
Matthew Harrison Perkal

SATURDAY, THE ELEVENTH OF JUNE, TWO THOUSAND SIXTEEN
AT THREE O'CLOCK IN THE AFTERNOON
Saint Patrick's Cathedral
BRIDGETOWN, BARBADOS

COCKTAILS AND RECEPTION TO FOLLOW
COBBLERS COVE • SPEIGHTSTOWN • BARBADOS
Formal Attire

Calligraphy: Everly Calligraphy | Illustration: Social Alchemy |
Photo: Charlotte Jenks Lewis

—121—

KELLY & STEFAN'S WEDDING STORY

BY KELLY VERSTRAETEN

Holding the philosophy that a marriage is a union where two individuals are intertwined yet separate
in identity, Kelly Verstraeten created an abstract watercolour play on two hues that move along together
in cohesion without creating a new colour. The logo was built on the same philosophy, melting "K" and
"S" nicely into a monogram then printed with gold foil. Modern and simple, a matching stamp seals
the envelopes as a finishing touch.

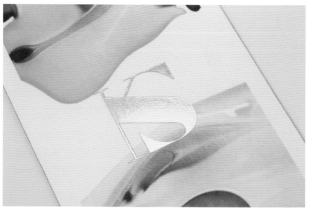

LECA & JULIANO

BY **GABRIEL FIGUEIREDO & GABRIELA SILVA**

For a couple who loves dressing in black, a wedding invitation with black-on-black aesthetics fits like a glove. Emphasising for their ceremony to be true to their own personality and values, this bold yet elegant invitation is infused with non-conformity and sophistication. Only a hint of gold, the monotone palette boosts slick class and minimalism.

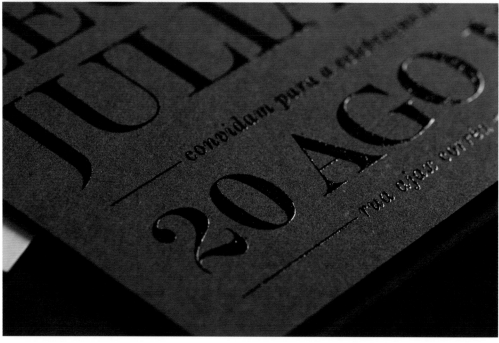

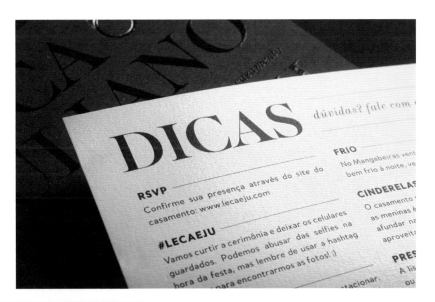

DICAS

dúvidas? fale com os noivos

RSVP
Confirme sua presença através do site do casamento: www.lecaeju.com

#LECAEJU
Vamos curtir a cerimônia e deixar os celulares guardados. Podemos abusar das selfies na hora da festa, mas lembre de usar a hashtag #LECAEJU para encontrarmos as fotos! :)

VÁ DE TÁXI
A rua é estreita, e pode ser difícil estacionar. Deixando o carro em casa, você garante mais conforto e tranquilidade para beber.

FRIO
No Mangabeiras venta bastante, e pode ficar bem frio à noite, venha preparado. (Sério!)

CINDERELAS
O casamento será no jardim. Nossa dica para as meninas é usar salto grosso (para ninguém afundar na grama), e levar chinelinhos para aproveitar a festa até o final.

PRESENTES
A lista está disponível no site do casamento, ou presencialmente nas lojas La Ville, Fast Shop, Tool Box, Vênica Casa e Espaço 670.

LECA & JU
rua ajax corrêa rabello 50
20/08 16H

CONVITE INDIVIDUAL
É INDISPENSÁVEL A APRESENTAÇÃO DESTE

GABI e GABRI

LECA & JULIANO

convidam para a celebração de seu casamento

20 AGO 16H

rua ajax corrêa rabello 50, mangabeiras

RENÊ & ALEX

BY **GABRIEL FIGUEIREDO** & **GABRIELA SILVA**

An accumulation of Renata and Alex's shared love for literature, travelling, and the arts,
the invitation design was inspired by their favourite author João Guimarães Rosa's collaborations with
artist Poty Lazzarotto. Both were also respectively from Minas Gerais and Curitiba, fitting the couple's
intention to represent themselves and follow their roots. Simple and elegant, its warm yellow indulges
in happiness and romance.

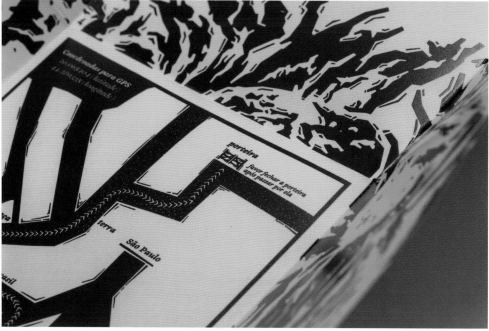

"Só se pode viver perto de outro, e conhecer outra pessoa, sem perigo de ódio, se a gente tem amor. Qualquer amor já é um pouquinho de saúde, um descanso na loucura."

Guimarães Rosa

Renata Ferri
— & —
Alexandre Sugamosto

Juntamente com nossas famílias, temos o prazer de convidá-los para a cerimônia do nosso casamento

—

dia 24/10 às 11:30 na
Fazenda Vista Alegre
em Igarapé (MG)
mapa no envelope

—

favor confirmar sua presença no site
www.sites.icasei.com.br/ferrisugamosto

Alex 41 9132 5552
Roseli 31 9949 5523
Renata 31 9633 3139

TOM & KARLIEN'S WEDDING INVITATION

BY JACQUES & LISE

Using the complementary colours of orange and blue, this quirky illustration stands out
in its energetic vibrancy. It balances both informal excitement with seriousness, seen in the active
dancing contrasting with the sincerity and quietness of the couple, capturing the essence of a wedding.
The gown merges with both the banquet and the dancefloor, tying all parts of the wedding into one.
Its handwritten words convey authenticity.

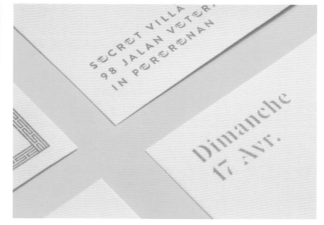

CAPUCINE & JERÔME'S WEDDING

BY JULIEN PRADIER

For this destination wedding in Bali, the invitation needed to excite guests about the exotic location and convey useful information about travel, activities and logistics. The flyers were printed as a four-colour Risograph to achieve a colourful effect inspired by Indonesian themes of patterns and shapes. A die-cut folder resembling Balinese wooden doors was designed to hold all the collateral.

Risoprinting: Ink'Chacha

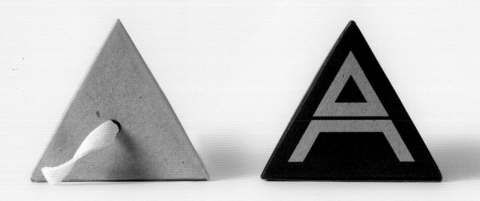

281214

BY LUMINOUS DESIGN GROUP

This invitation design is threefold: announce details of the couple's wedding, the christening of their child, and balance the three in equal representation. The triangular tube highlights the date in large typography and offers details on the poster held within. Through the use of craft material and bookbinding paper, the overall industrial aesthetic matches the warehouse venue's feel.

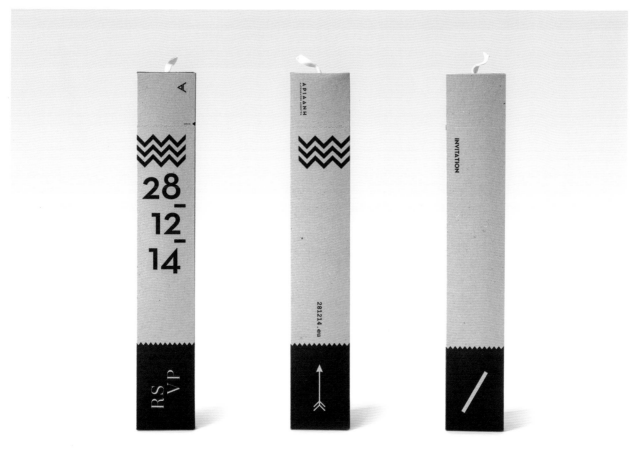

GEMEINSAM

BY MARIE PIERER

Taking on the word "together", or *Gemeinsam* in German, the central theme for this invitation is an infinite loop, characterising the notion of everlasting love and two people coming together. Inside the loop are the couple's names. As the couple's overall identity, this plays out in forms, ranging through embossing on the wedding invitation and in print on the RSVP card.

KIRCHLICHE TRAUUNG
Um 14.00 Uhr in der
Johanneskirche Klagenfurt,
Martin-Luther-Platz 1, 9020
Klagenfurt am Wörthersee

HOCHZEITSFEIER
Alte Schule
9162 Kappel an der Drau

P.S.: WEIL UNS WEIN UND
KÄSE DEN TAG VERSÜSSEN,
IST UNSER LIEBSTES
URLAUBSZIEL FRANKREICH.

DRESSCODE
Festlich & chic

RÉPONDEZ S'IL
VOUS PLAÎT
20.04.2017
—
+43 650 40 91 840

DETAILS
www.eva-max.at

03. JUNI 2017

GEMEINSAM

EVA & MAXIMILIAN

Photo: Alexander Krischner

DANIELLE + DEANE SAVE THE DATE

BY MELISSA DECKERT

Melissa Deckert has created the Save-the-Date notice for her friends' wedding. Informed by the couple's humour and interests, and the desire for it to feel lush to match the West Palm venue, a "Where's Waldo" concept was taken to hide personal details about their relationship in the card. Their blind cat and a BMX bike were all incorporated into the floral motif.

Art direction: Danielle Mitchell

KARIN + SONDRE

BY OLSSØNBARBIERI

Often when couples speak about love they say they've found their other half. Using this insight, the design of the invitation made sure the message will not complete without the other — recipients can only read the content when the cards are mounted together in the right way. Cut by hand and supported with an instruction paper, each half of the invitation reflects part of the couple's uniqueness — sky blue and Grotesque font for Sondre and ivory white and Didot font for Karin.

Photo: AJB Studio

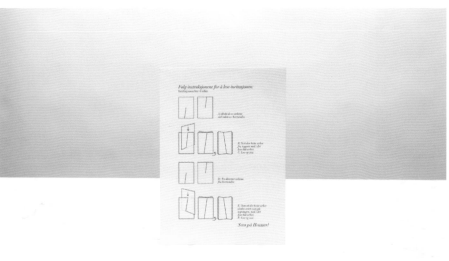

THE YEAR IN LOVE & THANKS

BY ORIGIN.DESIGN STUDIO

For their wedding invitation, the couple had in mind a message of love and appreciation to all those receiving it. While textures, typography and handmade elements were combined to convey warmth and joy, photos of the couple and a natural environment formed a consistent, personal backdrop to be overlain with text. The cards were hand-tied with twine and stamped with gold to add a feeling of elegance.

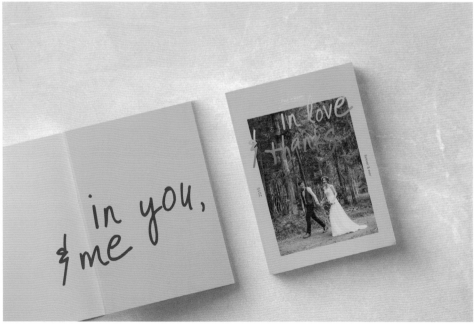

VENETIAN MYSTIQUE

BY PRATÌC DESIGN

When designing a bespoke wedding invitation for an Australian couple's wedding in Venice, a dramatic and romantic look and feel were used alongside iconic Venice imagery, like narrowboats. This treatment spanned across the printed materials from menu to the party favour packaging. Dramatic and rich colours infused passion into the set, while sealing wax and adorning ribbons added hand-rendered accents.

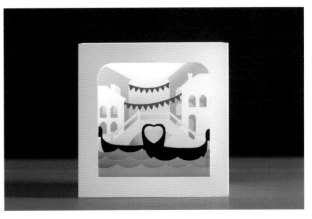

OLIVE TREE WEDDING CARD

BY SINCERELY,

Invoking the metaphor of an olive tree and its association for love, joy and peace, this wedding invitation includes many delicate features. Similar to the act of carving names into a tree to as a declaration of love, the main card is made from three different papers to mimic tree layers. Gold gilding on the edges adds shine, all wrapped in a brown pearl paper band with a dried eucalyptus tree leaf tucked in.

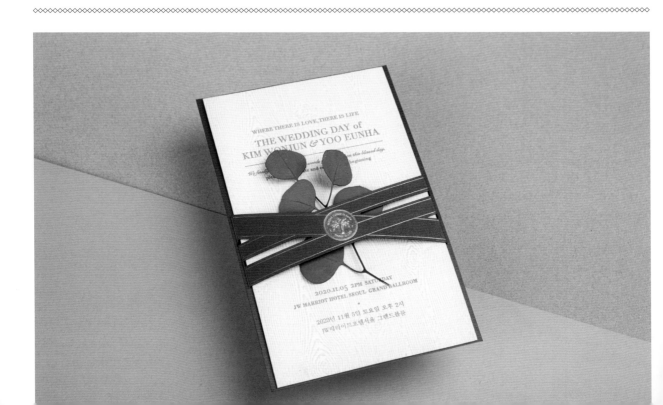

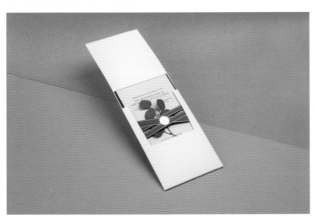

Who to organise your wedding

This can be a crucial, and sometimes, political decision! There will be no end of advice and offers, but ultimately it is your special day and the organisation of it should fall upon the best person to realise this. In the event of a possible permanent family rift, hiring a wedding co-ordinator is a sensible option.

It is important to keep in mind that whoever is paying for the bulk of the wedding should be involved in some of the planning. If the two of you are paying for it, then it is down to you two to choose if you wish to involve anyone else. It is considerate to invite parents along to see the venues, perhaps to the menu tasting, and they should certainly be present at the ceremony rehearsal. Brides often opt to involve their mother in the bridal gown and bridesmaids dress shopping. It is also considerate for you both to be involved in helping your parents choose their outfits.

If one set, or both sets of parents are contributing financially to your wedding, they may well expect more involvement in the planning. If you find this a daunting thought, prepare a to-do list early on and allocate jobs. This gives them defined roles and tasks which make them feel valued and helpful, and for you, you know that these tasks are being dealt with by (hopefully) reliable people!

If your family situation is one where you fear over-bearing intervention and opinion, it is wise to hire a wedding planner. The planner then becomes the liaison point and prevents you from having to field unwanted opinions and help.

OFF WE GO

BY X SPOTS THE MARK

Looking for an unconventional wedding invitation, Justin and Karen received a giant fold-out poster design full of illustrations of things they loved doing together. Alongside the invitation, postcards were sent to guests so they could fill them out with memories and wishes for the couple. Themed 'off we go', the entire design treatment alludes to the couple's next big adventure – marriage!

PENCIL US IN!

BY EMMA JO STATIONERY

A playful take on a Save-the-Date card formed part of the inspiration behind this invitation design. Sent off to guests complete with a real natural finish pencil individually painted in metallic foil, the ask from the bride and groom was simple: 'pencil us in', literally. The cards were printed on thick white board made from 60% recycled beer labels, matched with the vintage-style poster typography creating a vintage style aesthetic.

Photo: Anna Hardy

HARLOW

BY EMMA JO STATIONERY

Print studio Emma Jo drew on the flirtatious and rhythmic nature of 1920's Art Deco aesthetics to propose a design wedding theme. Bold geometric shapes mixed with a white and gold colour palette offer couples the ability to match print finishes with any budget or requirements. Tags adorned with gold eyelets were used for save-the-date cards. The seating chart featuring name cards hung tassels gives a fun nod to the flapper-era.

Photo: Holly Booth Photography, Jo Bradbury Photography

HEADSTART FOR HAPPINESS

BY DREAM GIANT CREATIVE

Framed by skyscrapers, Singapore's historic civic district by the river that backdropped the wedding informed this stationery's design. Illustrations of the bride and groom in their wedding attire were created in an Art Deco style, matched by invitations, with details all handwritten and scanned to achieve an overarching nostalgic sense. The idea continues to run across the fabric posters, bottle labels and gift tags, creating a coherent look for the day.

Photo: Marko Marinkovic

JUAN & LAURA

BY EL CALOTIPO

For Juan and Laura's wedding invitation, Spain-based studio El Calotipo has gone for an unconventional size of 10 x 15cm. Designed in two colours and printed on a thick ivory paper, the invitation features hand-rendered typography printed using letterpress plates. Each envelope has a same-colour printed label, die-cut to resemble a postage stamp.

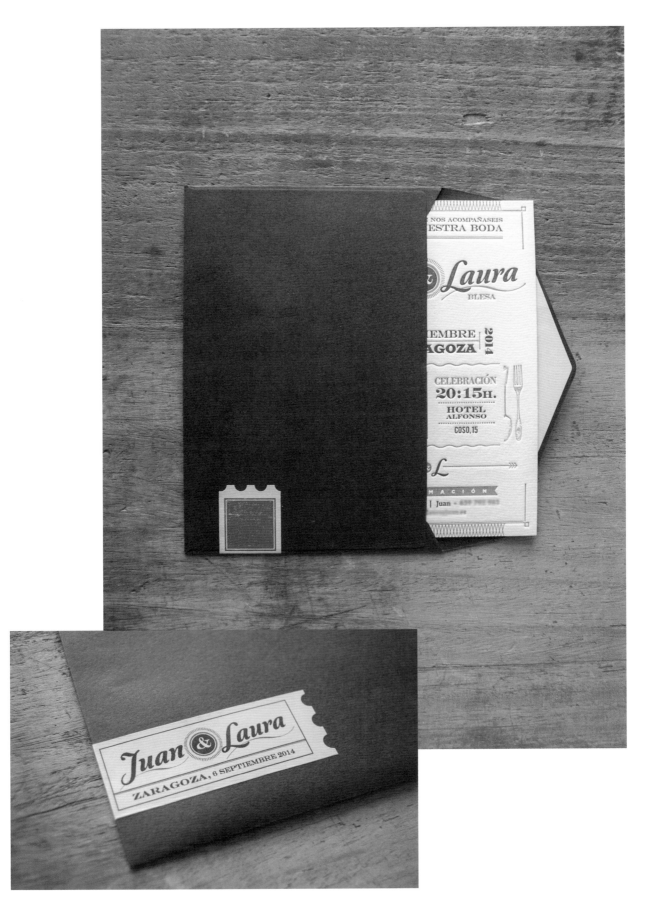

DEPAOLA WEDDING SUITE

BY RYAN DEPAOLA

Designer Ryan DePaola took on the task of creating the invitations for his own wedding to then-fiancé Celeste. With Downtown LA as the epicentre of their relationship, the cityscape forms the visual focus for the suite. Copper foiling, screen printing, letterpress and blind pressing were techniques used in this homage to the city and his partner.

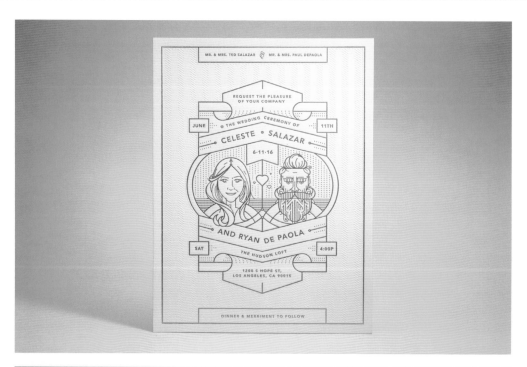

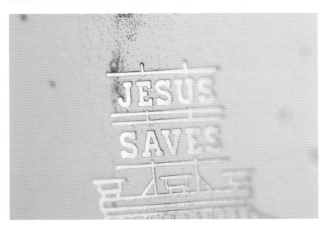

ASHLEY & MIKE

BY SHIPWRIGHT & CO.

A tribute to Ludwig Bemelmans, Bemelmans Bar in New York has its walls covered in the classic children's book creator's illustrations. To honour this place where the couple regularly spent their date nights, this wedding correspondence set captures the whimsical imagination of the multiple venues, hinted by the placement of each animal and plant. The invitations transition to a nighttime world, layered in three colours with the handwritten text filling up the full moon.

Photo & styling: Emma Kruch

CAITLIN & COLIN

BY SHIPWRIGHT & CO.

Colin and Caitlin's wedding stationery features a dreamy sun and mountains of Southern California where the two has planned to wed. From the orangey sunrise of the main card to the dark blue starry night on the thank-you card, the four colour scenes present the different stages and points of time of the wedding day. On the save-the-date, their son also appeared in Colin's favourite Miata, watching the sun rise with the couple.

Photo & styling: Emma K. Morris

COPPER WEDDING INVITATIONS

BY A FINE PRESS

With a notion to create a desirable design which guests would want to hold on to rather than throwing it away, this copper-stamped "card" will live on as an inspiring accessory. Adding a poster with a quote on the reverse, the invitation becomes a copper-framed letterpress print that could fit homes of any style. The oxidation of copper is guided to add moderate texture, contrasts and uniqueness to each of the cards.

Calligraphy: Emily J. Snyder

MOOC & CHIOU

BY HO TING-AN

Wedding is big business in the East. Correspondingly, the announcement should excite guests whilst also providing practical information about the day. Using red to reinforce the idea of happiness in Asian culture but slightly softened to make the cover more approachable, the bilingual display of the couple's names served to be inclusive to guests, showing the celebration is for all.

Illustration: Crystal Kung | Photo: Karren Kao

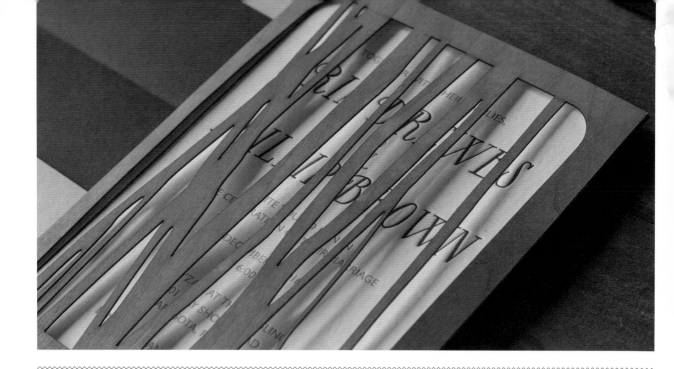

BANYAN TREE INVITATION

BY A FINE PRESS

The physical location of Erin and Phillip's wedding leant itself fittingly to their wedding invitation design. Literally in the shadows of ancient banyan trees, the notice is wrapped in a laser-cut wood sleeve peering out from behind the roots, creating a shadow effect and intrigue for guests attending. All hand-assembled, the invitations are meant to be kept and displayed as both a reminder and a tactile item of beauty in itself.

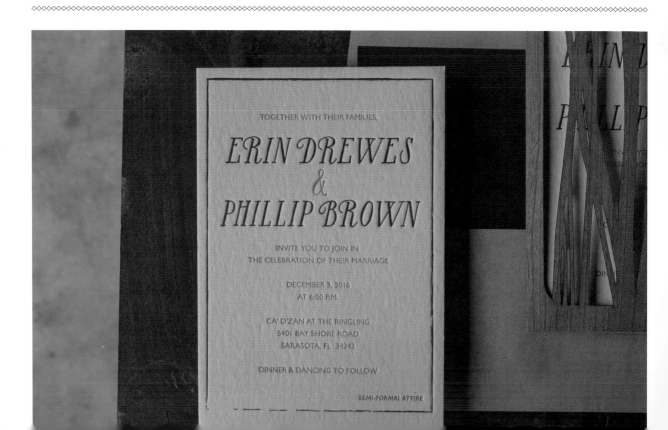

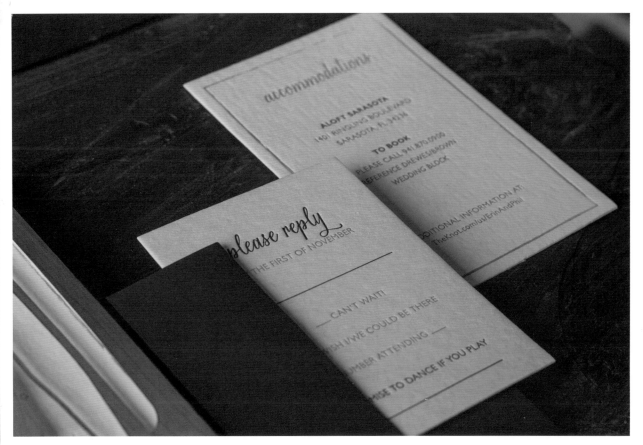

BRENNA WEDDING CORRESPONDENCE SET

BY RACHEL MARVIN CREATIVE

As part of a semi-customisable wedding invitation range, these vintage bird designs offer an unusual take to the classic invitation suite. Bold blues and a touch of blush pink tones form a pattern with crisp lines, giving a geometric edge to the intricate pattern. Copper accents in the finishing and envelopes add an earthy and luxurious touch. Couples are able to individually personalise the invitations to suit their requirements.

SOUTHERN PEACH WEDDING
CORRESPONDENCE SET

BY RACHEL MARVIN CREATIVE

This original design from Rachel Marvin mixes vintage peach etchings with a couple's initials in a romantic lettering style. Set to compliment a southern, rustic wedding, the design has soft colourings on black and white making the peach motif stand out and provide a consistent visual language for all of the wedding stationery. The customisable monogram will add a personal touch at the top of all stationery.

MAE WEDDING CORRESPONDENCE SET

BY RACHEL MARVIN CREATIVE

Rustic floral patterns in pastel are the main feature of this botanical invitation set. The intricate detailing of the flowers stands out on the white coloured paper creating a clean, delicate look. Circles and squares provide a framing mechanism so that the text are lifted from the flowering background and become easier to read. Printed on a cotton cover paper, the stationery is tree-free, 100% biodegradable and offers an organic textured feel.

RECESSIONAL
This is Love

the | WEDDING PARTY

MAID OF HONOR
Haley Reynolds.....Sister of Bride

BRIDESMAIDS
Christina White.....Childhood Friend
Laura Wilkins.....College Roommate
Abigail Burns.....Sister of the Groom
Grace Lee.....Cousin of the Bride

BESTMAN
Michael Jenkins.....Best Friend of the Groom

GROOMSMEN
Patrick Macdonald.....Brother of the Groom
Eric Miller.....Childhood Friend
Anthony Grant.....College Roommate
Doug Patterson.....College Roommate

FLOWER GIRL
Mary Reynolds.....Niece of the Bride

MUSIC
the Mar Quartet

IN REMEMBERANCE
Theodore & Michelle Holmes,
Grandparents of the Bride

miss | **ANNE HEATH**

KINDLY REPLY
by March 2

M_____

ACCEPTS WITH ANTICIPATION   DECLINES WITH REGRET
            ○   ○

the
DETAILS

FOR ACCOMMODATIONS, DIRECTIONS, WEDDING
TRANSPORTATION AND ADDITIONAL INFORMATION,
PLEASE VISIT OUR WEDDING WEBSITE AT:

WWW.AURORA&HENRY.COM

AURORA WEDDING CORRESPONDENCE SET

BY RACHEL MARVIN CREATIVE

This contemporary wedding invitation suite uses bold, elegant flowers to create a classic timeless design. Using black and white as the base colours, the soft pinks and deep greens of the florals contribute a dramatic yet luscious effect while handwritten style typography gives a modern touch, accenting the RSVP card and envelopes. The range is custom made to order and covers all design needs, including programmes, menus and table numbers.

Ensure your day is nicely paced

Although you would like your day to last as long as possible, this does not work in practice. If the day goes on too long, guests will get bored or tired — and leave early. It's best to end the party before it fizzles out. Your drinks reception should be no longer than 90 minutes and dancing for up to three hours is plenty. A successful wedding is one that flows with guests never being bored, hungry or thirsty.

We have all been to events, shows or ceremonies and become bored because they have gone on too long and we feel obliged to stay. A wedding is no different!

A guide is to say that the whole occasion from start to finish should be between 8-10 hours. The variation in time is largely down to a little longer dancing and allowing time for guests to get between the ceremony and reception venue, if they are taking place at different locations. Here is an example:

3.00pm	Ceremony
3.45pm	Photos
4.00pm	Depart for reception venue
4.30pm	Drink reception
5.30pm	Group photos
5.45pm	Dinner called
6.15pm	Bride & groom announced in to the room
6.30pm	Dinner served
8.30pm	Speeches & cake-cutting
9.00pm	First dance
12.00am	Bride & groom depart

It is important that speeches are not too long, there is an appropriate amount of time to speak and still maintain everyone's attention and enjoyment. Some people are more adept at speaking and are not at all daunted at making a wedding speech. If this isn't the case, I always say keep it short, sincere, and don't try to be funny. A genuine, heartfelt speech is as well received as a hysterically funny and witty one. Don't feel the pressure to be what you are not.

As a general rule, father of the bride speaks for five minutes, the groom the same, and the best man for up to 15 minutes. Brides often choose to speak too, and this is usually after the groom and before the best man. Speeches usually take place at the end of the meal, but people often opt to have them take place before or during now. Again, if public speaking is not something you relish, I always suggest doing them before the meal, that way you can all relax and enjoy the meal with the fearful anticipation removed!

M&K WEDDING INVITATION

BY MARTA ŚLIWOWSKA

When creating the wedding invitation for her sister's wedding, Marta needed to distil the timeless symbol of Christianity throughout the design. Tiny gold particles on a smooth black finish paper gave an understated, classic tone. On the cover of the silkscreen hand-sewn invitations, the couple's names are displayed with the back containing two locked circles, representing infinity and the way that two people come together forever.

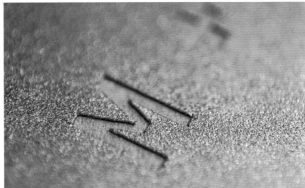

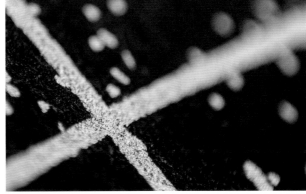

M&J WEDDING INVITATION

BY MARTA ŚLIWOWSKA

For her own wedding day, Polish designer Marta Śliwowska wanted to fuse together her and her partner's style and interests. Using an earthly colour palette, rustic elements and an off-beat stated typographic style, this mashup design aimed to create a balance between nature and design precision. The invitation was blind embossed and screenprinted on Bagdad brown and was hand-wrapped in felt jute with a feather accent.

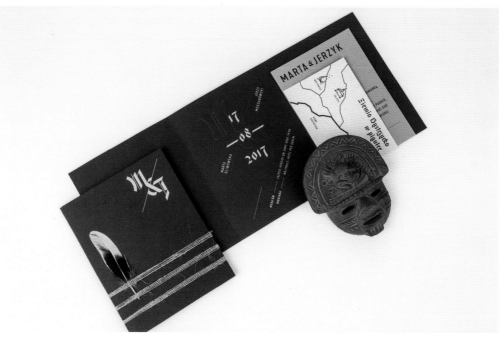

MARTA & JERZYK

PRAGNĄ ZAPROSIĆ

Ewę, Tatę i Dominikę

NA UROCZYSTĄ CEREMONIĘ ZAŚLUBIN
I MNIEJ UROCZYSTE BIESIADOWANIE POD CHMURKĄ.

PIĘKNĄ POGODĘ ZAMÓWILIŚMY, JEDNAKŻE,
JAK MÓWI GÓRALSKIE PRZYSŁOWIE — „ALBO PADAŁ
ALBO BĘDZIE PADAĆ!" RADZIMY WIĘC ZABRAĆ CO
CIEPŁEGO NA WIECZORNE HARCE PRZY OGNISK

PROSIMY O POTWIERDZENIE OBECNOŚCI
DO 17.07.2017 r. _____

Każdy grosik, który chcielibyście przeznaczyć
prosimy, by zasilił puchę dla potrzebu
ze schroniska dla

WEDDING IN SAVANNAH

BY STUDIO OF CHRISTINE WISNIESKI

Southern weddings in America are a colourful affair and designer Christine Wisnieski worked with her Cleverland clients to create vibrant country-inspired invitations for their big day. Bright orange turquoise hues at nearly full saturation drew out the linear pattern work, with die-cut polygons printed on Italian cotton paper. Slight grains in the colouring created a rustic and unique style while brown paper and envelopes provided an earthy grounding to the suite.

Styling: Dana Sobota | Photo: Paul Sobota

join us for a
WELCOME DINNER
THE LADY & SONS

—

see you in savannah

—

102 W CONGRESS STREET
5 O'CLOCK
coastal casual attire

GETTING HITCHED AT A FOOTBALL STADIUM

BY STUDIO OF CHRISTINE WISNIESKI

For a couple with a shared love for football that brought them together, these invitations has a playful game-like theme. Guests are given a play-by-play for the day's events that match the football environment set in Cleveland Browns stadium. Lucky number 13 representing the day the couple wed, is present throughout the designs, including hand held flags for the guests to wave. A ladylike colour palette was chosen to give a feminine feel, combined with a bold typography.

Styling: Dana Sobota | Photo: Paul Sobota

META & ALBERT

BY MONDO MOMBO

For Slovenian couple Albert and Meta, both lovers of nature, a strong earthy theme with elements of being in the woods was important. The wedding invitation has illustrations of the bride and groom in a forest setting and is part of a pack that offers a truly immersive natural experience. The box contains small holes so the scents of the moss and Marseille soap inside would waft out, evoking a feeling of the great outdoors.

Photo: Katja & Simon Photography

JACKIE & HARRY'S

BY SHINDIG BESPOKE

Set on the Island of Kauai, Hawaii, the brief for Jackie and Harry's wedding had no creative constraints aside from the need for the invitations to be colourful and unique. Textures and patterns were mixed together on a curly maple wood veneer card with the couple's name in a modern type treatment. Real moss was inlaid to give a tropical, living feel with a hot pint screenprinted heart and gold foiling to add depth and shine to the overall design.

Photo styling & florals: Belovely | Planner: Moana Events | Photo: Carina Romano, Love Me Do

STEPHANIE & ZACK'S AUTUMN WEDDING

BY SHINDIG BESPOKE

The brief for Stephanie and Zach's wedding was to use a bold colour and format whilst still portraying elegance and formality. The main card was printed with autumn floral patterns in four colours on cobalt blue. Designed in an origami style, the over-sized invitation unfolded from within the card, featuring gold foiling. The entire suite was packed in a translucent glassine envelope so the strong colours peered through, exciting guests upon receipt.

Photo styling & florals: Belovely | Photo: Love Me Do

MELISSA & GREG'S VINTAGE-INSPIRED WEDDING

BY SHINDIG BESPOKE

Melissa and Greg wanted an invitation that could match the industrial, rustic nature of their wedding venue, The Brooklyn Winery. To give the design a historic and tactile feel, Shindig screenprinted a wood veneer card with mixed bold types. Real photographs of the couple's grandparents were also brought together in a faded black envelope, lined with a vintage photograph of the Brooklyn Bridge to reference the area's past.

Photo styling & florals: Belovely | Photo: Love Me Do

DARYL & AMIR'S NEW YORK WEDDING

BY SHINDIG BESPOKE

With the Chrysler Building within view from their apartment, Daryl and Amir wanted to blend in their wedding invite the Art Deco style of the building with a current New York feel. Elements of the classic art movement including geometric shapes were clashed with a bold, mix of modern type and iconography. The medley of black, greys and whites gave an urban and classic treatment juxtaposing different eras of the great same city.

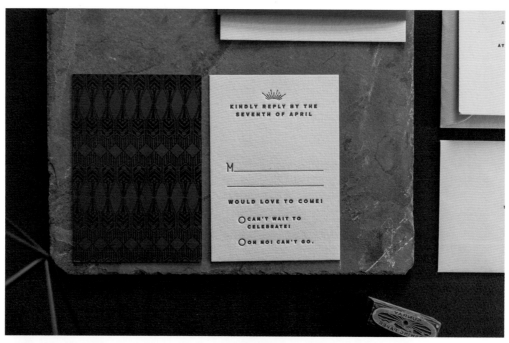

Photo styling & florals: Belovely | Photo: Love Me Do

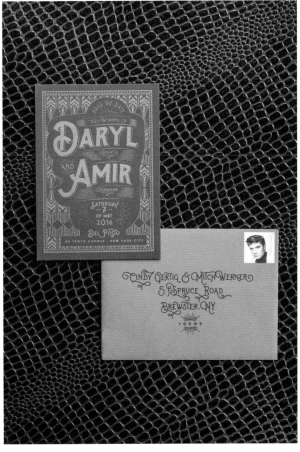

REBECCA & STEVE'S AUTUMN WEDDING

BY SHINDIG BESPOKE

Whimsically painted watercolour floras and fruits in bright harvest tones mixed with playful black type set the tone for this autumn wedding at the Horticultural Center in Philadelphia's Fairmount Park. While the wedding was a black tie affair, and so forest green envelopes, the classic black letterpress, and gold foil were brought to balance the light-hearted elements running all the way from the save-the-date through to the welcome packet and ceremony cards.

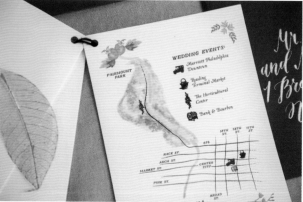

WANG & CHENG'S WEDDING INVITATION

BY ABINGO WANG

Breaking from convention of Eastern wedding traditions, Abingo Wang rid the invitations of vibrant red and gold, and opted for a peachy pink and silver foiling to symbolise sweetness. The simplified drawing of the dragon was an attempt to flip tradition and present an innovative format. The decorative lines provide the border with the square typeface completing this invitation.

Photo: Show Leejuan

MODERN BLACK & WHITE

BY CORAL PHEASANT STATIONERY

Coral Pheasant has created a classic invitation suite in black and white with modern typography, customisable to any couple's initials and specifications. Languid, flowing calligraphy adorns the outer envelope adding a touch of soft lines and delicateness. The bold type and minimalist design printed on thick quality paper offers an understated and classy layout, providing a sense of tradition and occasion for guests.

Photo: Carla Ten Eyck

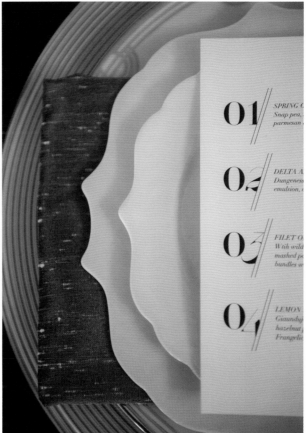

CHAMPS DE FLEURS

BY IDYLL PAPER

Using minimalist techniques, Idyll Paper have created wedding invitations for the thoughtful and refined. Playing on the floral aspects of weddings, wreath-like overflowing gardens provide a framing tool for text. Calligraphy and gold accents provide hints of enchantment whilst the soft paper edges and a muted ribbon provide the delicate finishing touches.

DOUCEUR

BY IDYLL PAPER

This collection of wedding stationery was designed with a focus on the subtle details. The range is named "Douceur", meaning 'softness', and is printed on natural paper with fluid, feathery edges giving an organic natural feel. Combined with embossing and floral patterns, the spacious layout and minimal calligraphy strokes aim to add texture and shades of romanticism.

Styling: Ginny Au | Flora: Ponderosa &
Thyme | Ribbon: Frou Frou Chic | Photo:
Erich McVey

ANNABEL & JONO

BY ATHENEUM CREATIVE

Crafted with the idea of bringing stories to life, Atheneum turned to maps as a way to show this couple's journey from their lives to their wedding. The invitations utilised a mixture of classic maps with calligraphy to demonstrate this. Using postcards as a reply provided a personal alternative to the usual card and envelope. All parts of the invitation were neatly tied together with string and a die-cut monogram of the couple's initials.

Photo: Chelsea Davis

CHRISSY & TOM'S BOHO WEDDING

BY SHINDIG BESPOKE

Chrissy and Tom were planning to make their vows at a plant nursery that formerly housed a mushroom farm. To make this celebration extra special, this invitation suite drew on the venue's history and connections to nature to create a warm, rustic vibe. Detailed botanical drawings, embossed grain texture and an earthy palette reinforced the idea with a sense of authenticity. The main card resembled a macramé wall hanging and evoked vision of a decent home.

Styling: Belovely | Photo: Love Me Do

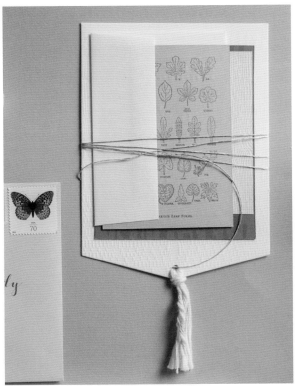

WEDDING PASS SET

BY STUDIO PROS

The wedding pass set was an invitation card created so that guests would feel like they were given tickets to attend the event. A smaller card affixed with string to the main invite was designed as a bookmark to remind guests of the date and show a map of where the venue was; each debossed with the couple's crest. Four different colours were used in the design, created for the different ages of guests, all adorned with a metallic type.

Photo: Shengyuan Hsu

C&H POP-UP WEDDING INVITATION

BY LI DYIN

Designed as both a flat and a three-dimensional invitation, this wedding card provides different perspectives on the big day. Showing portraits of the bride and groom in different settings related to their lives when flat, it projects memories in layers once folded into a cube. The heart in the middle connects the two, a symbol of their future together.

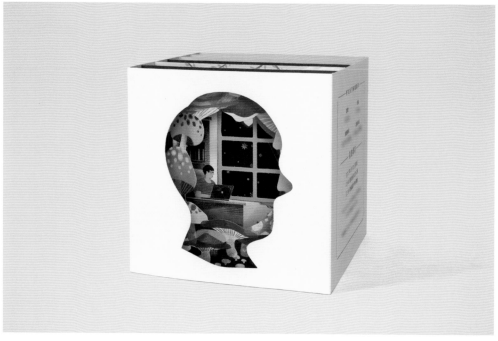

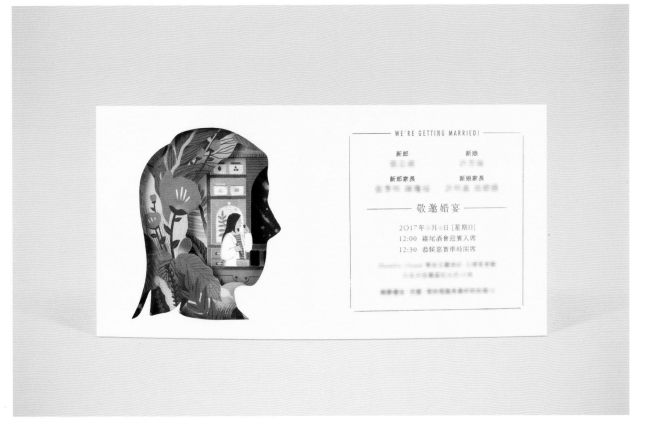

Studio Mondine
ON FLORAL ARRANGEMENTS

Anna Campbell Bridal
ON BRIDAL GOWNS

Chasewild Photography
ON PHOTOGRAPHY

Coral Pheasant Stationery
ON STATIONERY

De la Crème Creative Studio
ON WEDDING CAKES

NCh
ON BRIDAL ACCESSORIES

Getting it right
with Ivanka Matsuba & Amanda Luu
of Studio Mondine

After a successful wedding season working closely together, Amanda, a California native, and San Francisco transplant, Ivanka, decided to join forces in 2014 and beautify weddings and events with inspired blooms. Underpinned by rigour, the duo celebrates nature with rare blooms, the layers of seasonality and their affinity of simplicity, in naturalistic, nuanced palettes.

Are flowers an accessory? What significance do they hold in weddings?

Without getting too philosophical, we assert that flowers are not an accessory, but instead, an essential. They reflect the beauty and ephemerality of joy, and of life. As a result, flowers are particularly poignant within the context of weddings.

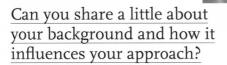

Can you share a little about your background and how it influences your approach?

We come from wildly different backgrounds (Ivanka from social work, Amanda from business marketing), but were shocked to find how synced up we were on all things aesthetic. We are drawn to the same poetry and elegance of the natural world. Our approach, thus, is to draw inspiration from the natural world first. Celebrating the unusual and rare, or the overlooked sidewalk weeds -- and usually, both side-by-side -- nothing is 'off-limits' in our designs. There is a tension in our work from negotiating a more lush, English garden aesthetic with the discipline of Japanese ikebana.

What trends in floral/botanical design do you see will dominate wedding celebrations?

We are excited to see more art- and concept-driven work coming from the wedding floral world. Our brides are requesting flowers that feel naturalistic and intentional, as though they were cultivated and plucked steps from the reception dinner.

"There's only so much 'pre-work' you can do before starting an arrangement... Once you start designing, though, let go and let the flowers lead."

What does it take to create a perfect bunch?

An incredible amount of care and consideration (and maybe a bit of obsessive compulsion) goes into creating flowers that look and feel effortless. Undertones, the balance of cool and warm, texture, finish...the list goes on.

Is there an awkwardly beautiful palette that definitely works but little would think of or dare to use?

If you follow our work, you'll notice there's a departure from our wedding flowers, which are client-driven, to our studio work. In the studio, when we are designing for ourselves, we are often testing new palettes and shapes. We'll often throw "challenge" palettes at each other, playing with colours that exist opposite each other on the colour wheel. Examples include soft tangerines and deep blues, or frosty lilac against a juicy, vibrant lemon.

What's useful to know before you start creating?

There's only so much "pre-work" you can do before starting an arrangement. Securing yourself ample time and ingredient variety is one thing. Once you start designing, though, let go and let the flowers lead.

Getting it right
with Anna Campbell of Anna Campbell Bridal

— MELBOURNE —

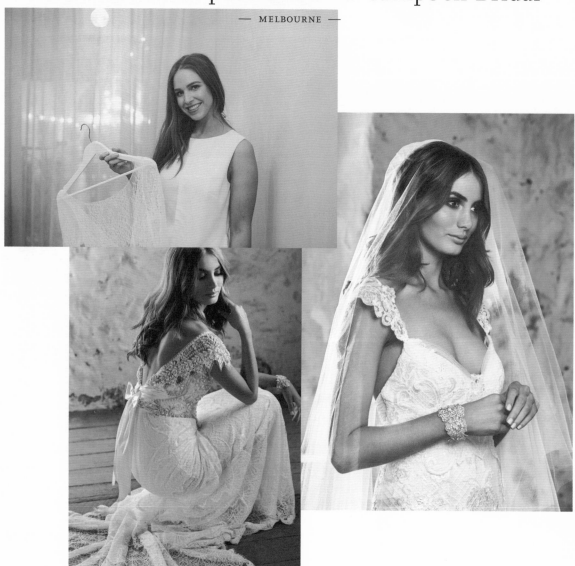

Marking its first decade as an Australian bridal Label in 2017, Anna Campbell and her eponymous brand have made a name for sending out vintage-inspired gowns and accessories. A champion of craftsmanship and a strong believer in creativity, the brand innovates and combines hand-beaded laces, natural silk and relaxed designs at their very own studio in Melbourne.

What is the one most important factor for a bride to consider when finding the perfect dress?

It's so important for a bride to feel like herself on her wedding day. This is true for the dress, but also hair and makeup, and even the kind of wedding she is planning. Sometimes a bride will have so many ideas that the search for the perfect dress can be overwhelming. In these cases, we like to sit down with our brides and learn about their style, their wedding plans, and the party size, etc., which would allow us to create a dress that is complementary to both her and the wedding's style. After all, we want our brides to have the most incredible time on their wedding day. If she is planning to get wedded on a beach, we might suggest a dress with a flowing silk skirt and a pair of hand-embellished footcuffs to wear with bare feet, instead of a fully-embellished fitted trumpet gown. Ultimately, a bride needs to be true to who she is, and what will make her feel her most beautiful and comfortable on her special day.

What are some trends you are noticing now and what are some past trends you would love to bring back?

The theme of botanical-inspired laces, bows and flowing silk skirts embroidered with delicate lace details are definitely the trends that we continue to see from lots of different designers' collections at the moment. Being a brand that has always made a feature of our own classic silk bows, we love the romance of these details. Outside of bridal fashion, we are also seeing a lot of brides choosing to carry beautiful lush foliage and natives, instead of the traditional bridal bouquet too.

How do you balance between trends, the Anna Campbell style, and the bride?

We have never been an 'on trend' label. We will always be Australian made, hand-finished in house, and use luxury fabrics, including silks, stunning laces, and intricate breathtaking beadwork. I think that is the perfect recipe for what a bride wants.

Our collections have expanded over time, but ultimately Anna Campbell has stayed true to who we are and what our brides love. We have never been too caught up with trends, as I think a wedding dress is something so special that it really should be true to who the bride is as a person and her own personal style. She should be able to look back on it in ten years and still love it just as much. So for us, while we are constantly working to perfect our designs and structures, we will always design vintage-inspired, romantic dresses to be hand-made in Australia, using only the most luxurious fabrics, sparkling hand-beaded embellishments and exclusive laces. This really is the Anna Campbell recipe for the perfect bridal dress, because it reflects exactly what our brides love to wear.

> *"All body types are different, and different brides will love different silhouettes on themselves... The most important thing is that our brides feel happy, comfortable and 'like themselves' on their wedding day."*

What is your opinion on brides going on diets to fit the dress instead of finding the dress to flatter their shape?

Admittedly this is a personal decision for every bride, but we would never encourage a bride to do this. All body types are different, and different brides will love different silhouettes on themselves – some might prefer a very fitted, trumpet skirt, whereas others love a soft, flowing silk tulle skirt. The most important thing is that our brides feel happy, comfortable and 'like themselves' on their wedding day. For this reason, we work with their stylist to find the best fabric and silhouette for the bride's figure and style, add extra hand-beading, raise a bust line or add definition to the waist to make sure our brides will walk down the alley in a truly unique gown that is perfect for that bride.

How do fabrics affect the look of the dress on a bride? Do certain fabrics and styles go well with certain body types and skin tones?

Fabrics are so important in any fashion design, but particularly in bridal. A wedding dress is such a special investment, and also an heirloom, and hence, we only ever work with the best natural silks and most beautiful laces. Even the lining of our dresses is completely silk, because it's the only fabric that feels truly luxurious against your skin, and we want our brides to feel like the most beautiful and glamorous version of themselves on their big day. Our team travels all around the world to source top-quality materials, bringing these back to our Melbourne studio where we hand-made every dress especially for each bride.

What do you do to help brides who are indecisive about what kind of dress they want?

While some brides don't know exactly what kind of wedding dress they want, they will know what their everyday style is – whether they like wearing strapless dresses, feel more comfortable with a sleeve, love sparkle and glamour, or prefer a demure lace. This is why we love to speak with our brides, to find out what they have regard for and the type of wedding they envision before selecting the designs that might suit. When a bride feels relaxed and excited in a dress, we know she has found the one!

Getting it right
with James Broadbent & Cameron Thorp
of Chasewild Photography

Regularly on the move chasing summers around the world, James Broadbent and Cameron Thorp seek to capture authentic moment of people in love. Since 2012, Chasewild has photographed couples in over 18 countries, from Morocco to Rarotonga, chasing after beautiful landscapes, lights and intimate moments.

How do you balance your own style while meeting a couple's vision?

We try to only accept bookings from couples who share the same vision for what makes a good wedding and what wedding photography is all about. When this happens we have full creative freedom to shoot what we consider is special, unique, and beautiful. This is what makes our work unique. Each and every wedding is inspired by our couples and where they choose to get married.

What do you think is essential in wedding photography?

For us, wedding photography is a combination of two key elements: storytelling and portraits that make you look stunning. Throughout the day we work hard to capture those small moments that often go unnoticed. We believe this is what any couple wants to remember from their day and it's what we are passionate about. This kind of documentary approach is really important for us and it works itself into every aspect of how we look at the day.

How do choose your locations? What effect can a location bring?

We spend a lot of time scouting out locations to shoot with our couples. It's really important that we have a location that looks absolutely stunning with perfect light so we can draw our attention to the couple without needing

"When you fully hand the reigns over to your photographer it allows you to sit back, relax and you can simply be yourself."

to work hard to make the light or location look great. Obviously, the locations that we use have a huge effect on the overall look of the images, we are looking for places with clean even light, diversity and somewhere that is totally unique so each of our couples has something that is special for their wedding images.

How do you prepare for a wedding shoot and get the best out of the couples?

Planning, planning, planning. We spend a lot of time working with our couples to ensure their timetable will work well — that we won't be stressed or running out of time during the

day and that we can shoot when the light is perfect. As mentioned above, we will always scout our locations beforehand, and we arrive early and check if the light will work for the ceremony. There's nothing more stressful for the couple (and ourselves) than a wedding that runs significantly behind schedule.

How do you make sure the couples appear natural in photo shoots?

We are *people people*, so this comes really naturally to us. We want our couples to enjoy every moment of the photo shoot so we spend a lot of time building a relationship with our couples so they feel comfortable with us. When we head out to shoot nothing is too serious, we keep things light-hearted and fun while also allowing the couple the space to enjoy some intimate time on their wedding day.

When we meet our couples we want to be sure that they are booking us because they absolutely adore our work and have full faith in our work. When you fully hand the reigns over to your photographer it allows you to sit back, relax and you can simply be yourself.

What trends are you noticing regarding wedding photography?

There are a lot of trends that come and go. Our goal is to create timeless images that our couples will still love in 20 years. A lot of the photography trends you see are in editing styles. When it comes to editing we want things to look natural and a true representation of what the day and location really looked like.

Getting it right
with Nichole Michel of
Coral Pheasant Stationery

— NEW HAVEN —

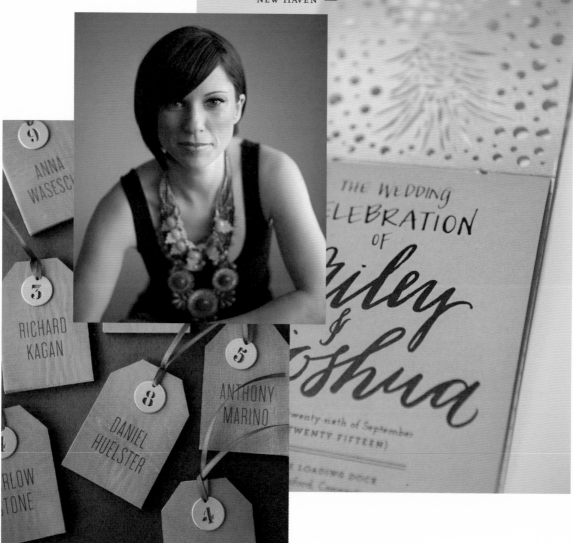

Proud to call herself a 'paper nerd' and with a BFA from the University of Connecticut, Nichole Michel spent eight years in corporate design before turning her hand to her stationery business. Located on the Connecticut shoreline, Coral Pheasant adores clients who respect etiquette but are also ready to break a bit of the rules to create personalised celebrations.

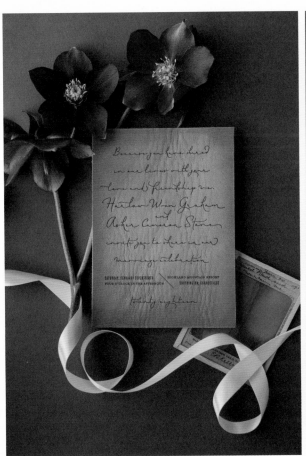

How many things can go into a wedding invitation suite?

The essential components of a classic invitation suite are the invitation, outer envelope, reply card and reply envelope. The invitation is the star of the suite. It sets the stage and formally announces your wedding. The reply card is the card your guests return indicating if they will or will not attend. Many couples choose to add additional pieces to their suite – for practical and visual purposes. For example, a website card may be included to guide guests to the couple's wedding website to learn further details about the celebration. An envelope liner is a detail often added to bring additional colour or pattern to the suite.

What draws you to focus specifically on wedding invite design?

Creating custom wedding invitations gives me the opportunity to always be designing something different from one project to the next. Each couple has a unique vision for their wedding day and I love being able to bring it to life. One couple might want an invitation that has a more traditional style and the next couple might be all about bold colours and modern design.

WE DO HOPE THAT YOU CAN MAKE IT, BUT WE UNDERSTAND IF YOU ALREADY HAVE A PRESSING
ENGAGEMENT. KEEP OUR HANDSOME, SMILING FACES IN MIND AND KINDLY LET US KNOW BY TH

the eighteenth of January

MOST DECIDEDLY YES! ⃝ \ WOEFULLY DECLINES
EXUBERANTLY ACCEPTS ⃝ SADLY NO.

Mr. and Mrs. Joshua Sullivan
43 Caledonia Road
Asheville, North Carolina
2 · 8 · 8 · 0 · 1

Because you have shared
in our lives with your
love and friendship we.
Harlow Wren Graham
and
Asher Cameron Stone
invite you to share in our
marriage celebration

SATURDAY, FEBRUARY SEVENTEENTH   HIGHLAND MOUNTAIN RESORT
FOUR O'CLOCK IN THE AFTERNOON   SOUTHINGTON, CONNECTICUT

twenty eighteen

DRESS AS YOU WISH
DINE AS YOU LIKE

dance
as you
please

FOR FURTHER DETAILS VISIT
WWW.HARLOWASHER.COM

USA 32

Southern Magnolia

POSTMASTER   DELIVER TO

Harlow & Asher

SEVENTEEN WINDSOR LANE
NORTH BRANFORD, CONNECTIC
0 6 4 7 1

Aren't Evites more environmentally friendly and convenient to use?

You can't argue with the ease or convenience of Evite. They're quick and affordable too. However, weddings are one of the few events where people still go through the process of designing, assembling, and mailing printed invitations. It's an age-old tradition that is nostalgic, personal and exudes a sense of formality befitting such a monumental celebration. Printed invitations certainly come at a higher cost, but it's an investment in elegance. Receiving a beautiful, thoughtful wedding invitation in the mail is the first glimpse guests get of the couple's wedding. The invitation sets the tone for the entire event and you want your guests to know that this is a party not to be missed!

What are the traditions to keep and rules to break for an on-trend design?

The wording on the main invitation should follow the traditional rules of etiquette and include the full names of the couple marrying and those of the hosts if they're different, the date, time and place. In that vein, a couple's wedding website should never be included on the main announcement. That detail should go on a separate enclosure card. At Coral Pheasant, we encourage clients to break the rules just a bit to create highly personalised celebrations. Perhaps the

invitation is letterpress printed on double-thick coloured stock (instead of classic white) and the enclosure cards are flat printed on complementary paper. Another "breakable" rule is to forgo reply envelopes – instead guests can be directed to reply via the couple's wedding website or email address.

What is the usual process for personalised invitations?

All of our design projects start with a complimentary consultation via phone, email or in person at our studio. Prior to chatting, we provide a questionnaire to learn more about our couple's vision and the celebration they are planning. During our consultation, we discuss all of the options, budget, style and preferences in detail. If meeting one-on-one, paper samples will abound and couples have the opportunity to see and touch a variety of papers, envelopes and print methods. We find inspiration in personal details and strive to create stationery that's as special as the couple. We encourage clients to come with magazine tears, photos, colour swatches, cherished heirlooms – anything that helps paint a picture of their big day and gets us on the same page.

carla & adam
11825 SUNSET CIRCLE
TELLURIDE, COLORADO
8 1 4 3 5

WOO HOO!

WE CAN'T WAIT TO CELEBRATE WITH YOU!
KINDLY REPLY BY AUGUST 12

M _____

But of course, dear!

With tears, no.

TOGETHER with their FAMILIES

riley & joshua

INVITE YOU TO THEIR
FUN-FILLED WEDDING EXTRAVAGANZA

SATURDAY **26** SEPTEMBER

{TWENTY FIFTEEN}
four o'clock in the afternoon

THE LOADING DOCK
375 Fairfield Avenue • Stamford, Connecticut

riley & joshua
438 SILVER BROOK ROAD, WESTPORT, CONNECTICUT
06880

WHAT'S THAT?
YOU WANNA KNOW WHERE THE PARTY'S AT?
VISIT OUR SITE FOR ALL THE INSIDE SCOOP!
www.rileyandjoshua.com

STATIONERY ——

—— *meet* CORAL PHEASANT STATIONERY

PINEAPPLE
JUICE

ICED CAKE
VODKA

PINEAPPLE
UPSIDE-DOWN
CAKE SHOT

MELISSA & ROBERT

INVITE YOU TO JOIN THEM IN CELEBRATING
LOVE, FAMILY, FRIENDSHIP AND MARRIAGE

SATURDAY

JUNE
21

2014

SIX IN THE EVENING AT THEIR HOME
THREE STONY POINT WEST, WESTPORT, CONNECTICUT

Casual Cocktail Attire

PLEASE

SAY YOU'LL ATTEND BY

JUNE 1

M

CAN'T WAIT! ◎

SORRY, CAN'T MAKE IT. ◎

BIRGE

THREE STONY POINT WEST
WESTPORT, CONNECTICUT
06880

What are the Dos and Don'ts when it comes to wedding invite design?

When beginning the process of wedding invitations:

• Do decide on a stationery budget range. That will help guide you in choosing from the many design and production methods that are the best fit.

• Do allow plenty of time to have your invitations designed and printed. Custom invitations should be ordered 6-8 months ahead and mailed 2 months before the wedding day.

• Do consider your colour scheme and invitation style. Your invitation sets the tone for your wedding and should reflect the style and feel of your actual celebration.

• Do order extra invitations and envelopes. More than likely you will need more of them than you think, and the cost of ordering extra is far less than placing a new order.

•• Don't use a married monogram on your invitations before you are officially married. Instead, use just your first initials.

•• Don't forget to stamp the response cards. It is a simple courtesy to your guests.

•• Don't include registry information on your invitation. Because giving wedding gifts is never mandatory, though the vast majority of attendees will naturally want to do just that.

*"It's an investment in elegance...
The invitation sets the tone for the
entire event and you want your
guests to know that this is a party
not to be missed!"*

Getting it right
with Heidi Holmon of
De la Crème Creative Studio
— SAINT LOUIS —

De la Crème Creative Studio's cakes are staggering beautiful whilst equally fabulous to eat. An autodidact cake artist, Heidi Holmon took a leap from her designer career in 2010, and channels her passion for colour, form, and texture to craft cakes at her studio in Saint Louis, Missouri, US. Since her first cake, her shop has won a dedicated following hunting for perfection.

Tell us about embracing wedding cake design as art.

Coming from a creative and talented family, art has always had a special and very natural place in my life. I see the world around me as a canvas on which to create. Cake is simply the medium that I use to express myself. Creating a masterpiece that looks too good to eat, that just happens to be insanely delicious, definitely satisfies the artist in me.

What trends in cake design do you see will dominate wedding celebrations?

Not following the trends within the industry is what got me where I am today. Trends change season to season, however, true innovation cannot be imitated. I've found that the modern couples are looking to add that tailor-made feeling to their special day, so they are looking for cake artisans who can design a wedding

cake as unique as their personal love stories. Whether I'm incorporating unusual botanicals or layering monochromatic textures, each cake is designed with an individual client in mind, and that is a trend that I would love to see stick around!

Were you professionally trained to craft cakes? How did your background impact your cake design?

Designing wedding cakes is something that happened quite accidentally for me, so I have no professional training at all. Being a self-taught perfectionist with an eye for detail freed my creativity and allowed me to focus on mastering the skills that I wanted to showcase. Setting my own styles rather than following trends is a direct result of this self-taught journey.

What's useful to know before you start creating?

I have a very thorough consultation process for wedding cakes and I like to hear as many details as possible. Some couples have an idea of what they want, but talking through everything, from the calligraphy on the invitations to the intricate detailing on the wedding dress, opens up a world of possibilities. You never know what little detail will spark the creative process.

Describe a cake that you've been dreaming to make.

I love to deliver the WOW to an event. While I've created some gorgeously decadent cakes, there is always room for one more in my portfolio...and I have a few ideas that are fit for royalty!!

What wedding cake elements do you like to pair together and why?

I'm not going to lie, I do have a favourite design aesthetic... I absolutely LOVE designing with a limited colour palette and clean lines! The fewer the colours, the better. Give me one or two neutrals, or a soft pastel paired with a metallic, and I am in heaven! There is something so stunning about quiet beauty.

"*From the calligraphy on the invitations to the intricate detailing on the wedding dress... you never know what little detail will spark the creative process.*"

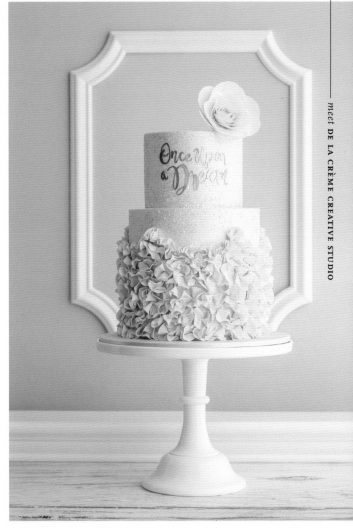

Getting it right
with Nastasya Klientova of NCh
— MOSCOW —

Describing herself as "incorrigible dreamer", Nastasya Klientova draws inspirations and searches for connections in simple things and the astonishing range of raw emotions of love. The nature of love, mainly rooted in her own wedding, provides an inexhaustible source of ideas for her bridal collections that has kept NCh going for many years.

What separates wedding jewellery from other jewellery in terms of style and design?

Wedding jewellery is beautiful and an exceptionally important detail of the bride image but not all girls think about it. For me, earrings are an essential element for a bride. You can skip every other kind of jewellery but the earrings.

The jewellery design can even be part of the wedding decoration. Should we approach the choice of wedding decoration with the same attention the bride gives to selecting her wedding dress? Definitely yes!

What is the right amount of accessory for a bride?

My character is fairly strong and I love exaggerated designs. I'm not afraid to offer massive decorations to brides. I freely manage colour and textures.

Can you share a little about your background? How did it play into your designs?

I spent four years in art school and another six years in university with a diploma in interior design. For several years I have worked as an artist and my paintings were sold all over the world. My artistic education provides a strong background for my work, also as my taste and intuition.

You use natural imagery a lot in your designs. What do you love about them?

I love to use plant motifs and this is not surprising because nature is the greatest inspiration possible. I work with large plant parts or very small ones, and often a combination of both.

What factors should be considered when choosing accessories?

When it comes to choosing accessories, a bride should clearly understand what style she wants to dress. It is necessary to pay attention to the dress' embellishments and the weight of the fabrics. For example, if the dress is made of chiffon or silk, it is better to choose a simple wreath made of small beads of cut glass and pearls, or a small ornate crown. If your dress is made of dense, heavy fabric, do not be afraid to go for massive ornaments, voluminous wreaths, scallops, crowns of large beads and metal. Remember one rule: if the dress is loaded with decoration, the jewellery must be simple and concise, and vice versa.

Crowns can and must be different. When making the crown, not only should the bride factor in the style, colour and decoration of the dress, but also her face shape and her characters. Crowns go with everyone. You just need to find your own!

How do you pick your materials and what kind of effect do different materials bring to the bride?

Each girl goes different, so I have a large selection of accessories in my arsenal. For example, for one bride I will collect jewellery from glass and pearls, and for the other I may go for massive decoration, which I take reference from vintage designer furniture. I constantly update my reserves and look for something new and unusual, because perfection has no limit.

"*The exclusive jewellery will complete the dress as much as possible according the character of bride and her dreams.*"

BIOGRAPHY

A Fine Press / Abingo Wang / Anna Campbell Bridal / Atheneum Creative / Chasewild Photography / Cheesiness Photo / Coral Pheasant Stationery / De la Crème Creative Studio / Dream Giant Creative / El Calotipo / Emma Jo Stationery / Erin Wheat Co. / Gabriel Figueiredo & Gabriela Silva / Ho Ting-An / Idyll Paper / Jacques & Lise / Julien Pradier / Kelly Verstraeten / Li Dyin / Love & Adventures / Luke Liable Photography / Luminous Design Group / Maïlys Fortune Photography & Gregory Batardon / Marie Pierer / Marta Śliwowska / Martin Aesthetics Limited / Melissa Deckert / Mondo Mombo / NCh / OlssønBarbieri / ORIGIN.DESIGN studio / Pratìc Design / Rachel Marvin Creative / Raquel Benito Photography / Ryan DePaola / Shindig Bespoke / Shipwright & Co. / sincerely, / Studio Mondine / studio of Christine Wisnieski / Studio Pros / Suite Paperie / The Crawleys / Vitaly Ageev Photography / X Spots The Mark

A FINE PRESS

The dreamer behind, Matthew Wengerd elevates communications with an ancient machines and cutting-edge technology printing words and pictures on luxurious materials. Also a jazz bassist by education, Wengerd finds it like playing jazz while creating made-to-order stationery for clients.

ANNA CAMPBELL BRIDAL

Marking its first decade as an Australian bridal Label in 2017, Anna Campbell and her eponymous brand have made a name for sending out vintage-inspired gowns and accessories. A champion of craftsmanship and a strong believer in creativity, the brand innovates and combines hand-beaded laces, natural silk and relaxed designs at their very own studio in Melbourne.

ATHENEUM CREATIVE

Creative directed and owned by Melissa Broderick, Atheneum Creative was crafted with the idea of bringing stories to life through a unique branded experience. Established in 2011 in Charlotte , North Carolina the inspired boutique firm is largely focused on wedding and event branding, and all that is fun.

CHASEWILD PHOTOGRAPHY

Regularly on the move chasing summers around the world, James Broadbent and Cameron Thorp seek to capture authentic moment of people in love. Since 2012, Chasewild has photographed couples in over 18 countries, from Morocco to Rarotonga, chasing after beautiful landscapes, lights and intimate moments.

CHEESINESS PHOTO

The work name of Victor de la Cueva from Mexico City who is a pizza junkie, lovers to dogs, Netflix, roadtrips and cold beer. A true supporter to FC Barcelona, Longboards, Vans, José González, KEXP, and Outdoors. Cueva's favourites also include Sunday Dates, HIMYM, shity soffee, typographies, and 4:20.

CORAL PHEASANT STATIONERY

Proud to call herself a 'paper nerd' and with a BFA from the University of Connecticut, Nichole Michel spent eight years in corporate design before turning her hand to her stationery business. Located on the Connecticut shoreline, Coral Pheasant adores clients who respect etiquette but are also ready to break a bit of the rules to create personalised celebrations.

DE LA CRÈME CREATIVE STUDIO

De la Crème's cakes are staggering beautiful whilst equally fabulous to eat. An autodidact cake artist, Heidi Holmon took a leap from her designer career in 2010, and channels her passion for colour, form, and texture to craft cakes at her studio in Saint Louis, Missouri, US. Since her first cake, her shop has won a dedicated following hunting for perfection.

DECKERT, MELISSA

Deckert is a multi-disciplinary designer and artist based in Brooklyn, New York.

DEPAOLA, RYAN

DePaola is an illustrator from Los Angeles now working and living in San Francisco as a senior brand designer for Weebly.

DREAM GIANT CREATIVE

A creative studio specialising in illustration, lettering and design. Dream Giant Creative loves naps but they are very creative when they are awake.

EL CALOTIPO

A design studio specialised in graphic design, web, identity, stationery, invitations, business cards etc. while also a printing studio for theor own works and clients including freelancers and other studios from all over the world. Their printing service covers letterpress, stamping, silkscreen, bookbinding, engraving, to name a few.

EMMA JO STATIONERY

Established in 2009 by designer Emma Prescott to provide a friendly, relaxed experience for couples that want something a little less ordinary with character and personal style. The small print studio is dedicated to good, honest design for paper lovers. We offer a diverse and ever expanding collection of wedding stationery. They are on endless pursuit of new, exciting techniques and concepts, specialising in bespoke designs and a variety of print options including letterpress, foil, digital printing and laser cutting.

ERIN WHEAT CO.

Wheat is an artist and journey woman passionate about the power of love as well as preservation and protection of the planet. Founding her company, Erin Wheat Co., at 19, she has photographed lovers across the USA and abroad besides working alongside numerous outdoor companies.

FIGUEIREDO, GABRIEL & SILVA, GABRIELA

Figueiredo and Silva met in college and have been together ever since. Throughout their career, they have followed different paths and interests, which always bring something new to their collaborative work.

page 124-127

HO, TING-AN

Born in 1991, Ho is an graphic designer and art director based in Taiwan. The award-winning designer is one of the most influential young gun designers in Asia, receiving numerous recognitions including Golden Butterfly Award, Design Awards Asia and iF Design Awards. His work is exhibited in Design Centre of Singapore, La Biennale di Venezia, Tokyo 21_21 design sight, etc. Graduated from Shih Chien University in 2014, Ho established STUDIO 411 in the same year.

page 166-167

IDYLL PAPER

Directed and owned by Tara Spencer, Idyll Paper is a stationery line for the thoughtful and refined. Taking an artful approach to wedding paper, the studio strives for effortless design that blends minimalist sensibilities with lush romanticism.

page 204-207

JACQUES & LISE

A couple as well as a creative inseparable duo from Belgium. For several years now Jacques and Lise have been closely working together as a freelance team, engaging themselves in a wide array of graphic design and illustration projects. They see each project as a new challenge in which they can attempt to surprise with a sense of style, concept, originality and eye for detail.

page 128-129

LI, DYIN

Born in 1991, Li Dyin is a graphic designer and illustrator based in Taiwan.

page 214-216

LOVE & ADVENTURES

Joie de Vivre sums up why Amy Scaife loves to shoot weddings and her approach. The all-ages exuberance, the gathering of all the strands of a couple's lives, weaving together through dancing, stories and laughter, drawing everybody tighter not only to the couple but to each other. For Scaife, the best weddings are not only love affirming, but community and life confirming.

page 80-85

LUKE LIABLE PHOTOGRAPHY

Born and raised in Saskatchewan, Liable lives and works in Victoria BC but also available world-wide. Liable is great at capturing moments in an emotional, creative, and organic way to tell a story or spark a memory.

page 48-55

LUMINOUS DESIGN GROUP

An Athens based storytelling studio providing services include branding, identity, print and digital design, packaging design and creative direction. Luminous Design Group creates expressive, bold and innovative communication, helping brands empower their vision through meaningful design solutions.

page 132-133

MAÏLYS FORTUNE PHOTOGRAPHY & GREGORY BATARDON

Based in Switzerland, Maïlys Fortune and Gregory Batardon are a couple working together as wedding photographers. Their style is a mix of photojournalism and fine art photography.

page 34-41

MARTIN AESTHETICS LIMITED

Love is like a stream of water. A camera has to capture the surging rhythms on the surface, but also the stillness underneath. Best pictures should likewise capture the different faces of love. Understanding the stories, experiences and values of a couple's subjects are must to achieve that. On some level, the photographer found that the actual level of photographic skill doesn't matter as much but his view of the world and attitude towards everything. Photography is a reflection of the heart.

page 42-47

MONDO MOMBO

Studio of Claudia Bordin where illustration has no boundaries and design resides on used and abandoned objects, with musical instruments and walls of camouflage rooms. Bordin follows projects and events that require customisation and creativity, offering unique, handmade, elaborate graphics, illustration and packaging products.

page 188-189

NCH

Describing herself as "incorrigible dreamer", Nastasya Klientova draws inspirations and searches for connections in simple things and the astonishing range of raw emotions of love. The nature of love, mainly rooted in her own wedding, provides an inexhaustible source of ideas for her bridal collections that has kept NCh going for many years.

page 252-258

OLSSØNBARBIERI

A multi disciplinary design studio specialising in brand identity and packaging design with particular focus on wine and spirits, as well as culture and art industries. Founded in 2005 by Henrik Olssøn and Erika Barbieri with the intention of working independently and without compromises in regards to conceptual development and quality of execution,

OlssønBarbieri evolves by pursuing new standards of design through research and experimentation. Their projects range from brand creation, visual identity, illustration and packaging design to brand design strategy and creative direction.

page 138-139

ORIGIN.DESIGN STUDIO

A young and growing design studio based in Taiwan. ORIGIN.DESIGN values highly on the interactions between clients and audience. The team studies and listens to clients' vision, observes and comprehends audience's need. Such intangible values are transformed into visual images through unique viewpoints and rich experiences. To them, pictures always speak louder than words, so they always try to build a connection between audiences and clients through designs that back to the origin.

page 140-141

PIERER, MARIE

Pierer born in 1990 in Graz, Austria. Studied photography at Akademie für angewandte Fotografie" and graduated in graphic and communication design from the HTBLA-Ortweinschule, Pierer started out as a make-up artist and later worked at moodley brand identity in Graz for four years. Pierer is now a freelance designer.

page 134-135

PRADIER, JULIEN

A French artistic director, Pradier specialises in visual communication crafted with passion, working alongside with clients from initial brief to product delivery, taking every step together throughout the way. When not working on commissioned projects, Pradier enjoys experimenting through various media. He always look for a visual balance between the realistic, the creative, and the abstract.

page 130-131

PRATÌC DESIGN

A Rome based creative studio with a particular love for all things hand-crafted and high quality paper creations that come along with actual touching, marking and folding. While everyone is aided by some of the latest technology, Pratic Design strongly believes in creating with passion while employing traditional techniques. Their love for timeless paper craftsmanship marks the starting point and is the basis of every project they do.

page 142-143

RACHEL MARVIN CREATIVE

A design and print studio specialising in fine wedding invitations and event stationery. Using age-old mediums and vintage inspired art pieces combined with bold typography and clean design, Rachel Marvin Creative creates refreshing and contemporary pieces that still contain that touch of classic timelessness. All products are made to order and printed at the studio located in historic Richmond, Virginia.

page 170-177

RAQUEL BENITO PHOTOGRAPHY

In his 30s, Benito was born in Barcelona, Spain with an artistic and crafty family. Knowing from a young age about his passion in photography, Benito began image studies in Barcelona and mastered in documentary photography at Efti Madrid. Started to shoot for weddings in 2010, Benito won an European prize as revealing photographer in 2013 which opened doors to best wedding planners and professionals of the sector. Benito currently teaches and lectures about wedding photography. He works internationally in countries such as Mexico, France, Italy, Greece, Germany, UK and Australia.

page 72-79

SHINDIG BESPOKE

Shindig Bespoke delights in creating unique, whimsical, colourful and fun invitations as well as related event tidbits in cohesive graphic style. Born of the idea that an invitation should be uniquely characteristic of each event it's announcing, the team invites clients to adventure and collaborate together! They love exploring all types of media, printing method and even materials. Shindig was inducted into the The Knot's Best of Weddings Hall of Fame in 2017 and is a seven time nominee and four time winner of The Greeting Card Association's Louie Awards for excellence in stationery design.

page 190-199, 210-211

SHIPWRIGHT & CO.

The studio of two old friends, Jen Kruch and Jessie Alberts, who share a love of art, design, coffee, food, and letterpress printing. Shipwright & Co. was born in 2013 with the support of a new-style Chandler and Price circa 1911, as well as a Challenge brand manual guillotine paper cutter. Housed in a small garage in an especially lovely nature of Napa, California, the studio is very mindful of being environmentally conscious using low-VOC rubber-based inks, vegetable oil and other natural products to clean their press, plus 100% cotton, tree-free paper recognized by the EPA as a recovered fiber.

page 160-163

SINCERELY,

A premium invitation boutique in Seoul, Korea. As the denotation of its name, the studio works with sincerity by picking the best quality of materials and by processing the uncommon printing nishings. They provide a large variety of choice in invitations on their website and customise the invitations and other stationery in countless ways according to customers' requests.

page 144-145

ŚLIWOWSKA, MARTA

From southwest Poland and mastered in graphic design at the Academy of Art and Design in Wrocław, Poland, Śliwowska is an independent graphic designer specialising in brand identity, logo design, editorial and signge. Śliwowska's clients include Necon and Kolektyf, as well as European Capital of Culture Wrocław 2016.

page 180-183

STUDIO MONDINE

After a successful wedding season working closely together, Amanda Luu, a California native, and San Francisco transplant, Ivanka Matsuba, decided to join forces in 2014 and beautify weddings and events with inspired blooms. Underpinned by rigour, the duo celebrates nature with rare blooms, the layers of seasonality and their affinity of simplicity, in naturalistic, nuanced palettes.

page 218-223

STUDIO OF CHRISTINE WISNIESKI

Wisnieski is a multi-disciplinary designer practice based in Cleveland, Ohio. Specialised in creating hospitality brands, Wisnieski's work has been honoured by AIGA, Print Magazine, and Communication Arts. It has been featured in Better Homes & Gardens, Design*Sponge, ELLE Decoration Sweden, The Huffington Post, Kate Spade, Ladies' Home Journal, and Martha Stewart.

page 184-187

STUDIO PROS

Studio Pros is a design studio directed by Li Yi-Hsuan from Taiwan. The studio focuses on print and screen based design working on projects about dranding, typography, packaging, web and app design.

page 212-213

SUITE PAPERIE

A NYC and Ridgewood based design studio that specialises in creating custom suites for weddings, events and businesses. From invitations, note cards and announcements to logos, letterhead and business cards, Suite

Paperie believes that every wedding, event or brand is worthy of impeccable, smart designs and flawless printing. They offer various types of printing in order to accommodate almost all budgets and they pride themselves on thinking outside of the box and attention to detail.

page 118-119

THE CRAWLEYS

As international award winning husband and wife team of Bee and Liam from England. Liam is the man behind the camera and Bee is tucked away in digital darkroom working on images. With over 15 years of history, The Crawleys has been part of over 500 weddings, and has won many awards - most recently The Wedding Industry Awards UK Wedding Photographer of The Year 2017 and The Wedding Industry Awards North West Wedding Photographer of The Year 2017. They are also named as one of the top 150 photographers in the world through SLR Lounge, and to be included in Junebug Weddings hot list of top international wedding photographers.

page 100-109

VERSTRAETEN, KELLY

Graduated in graphic design at the Royal Academy of Fine Arts of Antwerp, Verstraeten did another postgraduate in brand and packaging development at Luca school of Arts in Ghent. Her work is built on the principles of strong concept, simplicity, clarity and character. With special focus on details, she creates real stories and uniquely identified designs for brands. Verstraeten is a typography, art and design enthusiast who likes to travel and discover the world.

page 122-123

VITALY AGEEV PHOTOGRAPHY

Ageev is a fine art wedding film photographer. Born in the south of Belarus in the city of Gomel, Ageev has taken a great interest in photography since the school years. With the course of time, his hobby has trans-

formed into a lifestyle. He also likes travelling, visiting new places meeting with new people, listening to the life stories and visualise them by means of pictures. Not only recording the instant moments but portraying the whole lifestory at the image. Ageev's photos are tender, airy and warm through the use of film camera that conveys a special atmosphere of the events.

page 110-115

WANG, ABINGO

Wang graduated from the Department of Applied Arts, Fu Jen Catholic University. His majored in visual communication design specialising in brand identity, package design, and typeface design. His works won numerous international awards, including Hiiibrand Awards and International Art and Design Association Award (IADA). Fond of rock music, Wang also loves to explore and share all things novel.

page 200-201

X SPOTS THE MARK

Fueled by the love of creative exploration, Xinnie Ng creates and concocts illustrative designs that brew and balance a love for the handwritten and digital. Born and bred in Singapore with a background in art, industrial design and intense people watching guide Ng's creative process and perspective. Expanding across different creative terrains, her past clients have included Deloitte Singapore, National Council of Social Services, Asian Civilisations Museum, Channel NewsAsia, as well as several start-ups and curiously courageous wedding folks.

page 148-149

ACKNOWLEDGEMENTS

we would like to thank all the designers and companies who have involved in the production of this book. this project would not have been accomplished without their significant contribution to the compilation of this book. we would also like to express our gratitude to all the producers for their invaluable opinions and assistance throughout this entire project. the successful completion also owes a great deal to many professionals in the creative industry who have given us precious insights and comments. and to the many others whose names are not credited but have made specific input in this book, we thank you for your continuous support the whole time.

FUTURE EDITIONS

if you wish to participate in viction:ary's future projects and publications, please send your website or portfolio to submit@victionary.com